a stolen life

a memoir

jaycee dugard

SIMON & SCHUSTER

New York London Toronto Sydney

Simon & Schuster
1230 Avenue of the Americas
New York, NY 10020

First Simon & Schuster hardcover edition July 2011

SIMON & SCHUSTER and colophon are
registered trademarks of Simon & Schuster, Inc.

For information about special discounts for bulk purchases,
please contact Simon & Schuster Special Sales at
1-866-506-1949 or business@simonandschuster.com.

The Simon & Schuster Speakers Bureau can bring authors
to your live event. For more information or to book an
event contact the Simon & Schuster Speakers Bureau at
1–866–248–3049 or visit our website at www.simonspeakers.com.

Designed by Joy O'Meara

Manufactured in the United States of America

10   9   8   7   6   5   4   3   2   1

Library of Congress Cataloging-in-Publication Data

Dugard, Jaycee Lee, 1980–
    A stolen life : a memoir / Jaycee Lee Dugard. — 1st ed.
        p.   cm.
    1. Dugard, Jaycee Lee, 1980—Kidnapping, 1991.   2. Kidnapping
victims—California—Biography.   3. Kidnapping—California.
4. Sexually abused children—California—Biography.   I. Title.
    HV6574.U6D84 2011
    364.15'4092—dc23
    [B]   2011018938

ISBN 978-1-4516-2918-7
ISBN 978-1-4516-2920-0 (ebook)

Dedicated to my daughters.
For the times we've cried together,
laughed together.
And all the times in between.

Author's Note

This book might be confusing to some. But keep in mind throughout my book that this was a very confusing world I lived in. I think to truly begin to understand what it was like, you would have had to be there, and since I wish that on no one, this book is my attempt to convey the overwhelming confusion I felt during those years and to begin to unravel the damage that was done to me and my family.

You might be suddenly reading about a character that was never introduced, but that's how it was for me. It didn't feel like a sequence of events. Even after I was freed, moments are fragmented and jumbled. With some help, I have come to realize that my perspective is unique to abduction. I don't want to lose that voice, and therefore I have written this book how it came to me naturally. I'm not the average storyteller . . . I'm me . . . and my experience is very uncommon. Yes, I jump around with tangents, but that's sometimes the way my mind works. If you want a less confusing story, come back to me in ten years from now when I sort it all out!

Jacyee Lee Dugard, age eleven

Introduction

Let's get one thing straight! My name is Jaycee Lee Dugard. I was kidnapped by a stranger at age eleven. For eighteen years I was kept in a backyard and not allowed to say my own name. What follows will be my personal story of how one fateful day in June of 1991 changed my life forever.

I decided to write this book for two reasons. One reason is that Phillip Garrido believes no one should find out what he did to an eleven-year-old girl . . . me. He also believes he is not responsible for his actions. I believe differently. I believe that everyone should know exactly what he and his wife Nancy were doing all these years in their backyard. I believe I shouldn't be ashamed for what happened to me, and I want Phillip Garrido to know that I no longer have to keep his secret. And that he is most certainly responsible for stealing my life and the life I should have had with my family.

I'm also writing my story in the hopes that it will be of help to someone going through, hopefully not similar conditions, but someone facing a difficult situation of their own—whatever that may be. It's easy for people to be horrified and shocked when someone is abducted, but what about all the other adults and kids living in sad homes? My goal is to inspire people to speak out when they see that something is not quite right around them. We live in a world where we rarely speak out and when someone does, often nobody is there to listen. My hope is that society changes in regards to how we treat someone who speaks out. I know I am not the only child to be hurt by a crazy adult. I am sure there are still the families that look great on the outside, but if someone were to delve deeper they would discover horrors beyond belief.

For many, it is so much easier to live in a self-made "backyard" that it can be tough and scary to venture out and leave that comfort zone behind. It is so worth it, though. You could be saving a person or a family who is not able to save themselves.

Take my case, for example: two Berkeley cops saw something amiss and spoke up about it. Even if they would have been wrong, they still did the right thing by speaking up. I will forever be grateful to them for doing the thing that I could not do for myself.

Back then, it was a struggle to get through a day, but now I look forward to each day and the next to come. After eighteen years of living with tremendous stress, cruelty, loneliness, repetition, and boredom, each day now brings a new challenge and learning experience to look forward to.

With my writings, I hope to convey that you can endure tough situations and survive. Not just survive, but be okay even on the inside, too. I'm not sure how I did endure all that I did. I ask myself less and less every day. I used to think maybe the one reading this would find the answer for me, but I am beginning to think that I have secretly known all along.

Ask yourself, "What would you do to survive?"

Me, J-A-Y-C-E-E, age two

My situation was unique, and I can't begin to imagine what others are going through in their daily lives. You can survive tough situations is all I can say. I did. History has taught us that even when it looks like there is no hope, hope still lives in people's hearts.

T. S. Eliot once wrote, "I said to my soul be still, and wait without hope; for hope would be hope for the wrong thing."

My trust and hope were indeed put in the wrong person(s), but nevertheless it still lived.

I am so lucky and blessed for all the wonderful things that I do have. Life is too short to think about all the things you don't have. I had my girls to give me strength and my cats to keep me warm at night and, perhaps deep inside, the dim hope of seeing my mom again. Even if it is just one thing or person you have to be thankful for, that is enough. Yes, I do believe I'm lucky. I could not have gotten through my ordeal without believing that some-day my life would make sense. Life's adventure is important. It is important to live each day to its fullest, whatever life brings you.

Me, feeling angry at age eight

First snowman

The Taking

It is an ordinary Monday morning school day. I have woken up early this morning of June 10th, 1991. I am waiting for my mom to come in my room before she goes to work to kiss me good-bye. I made a point the night before to remind her to kiss me good-bye.

As I lay in bed waiting, I hear the front door close. She has left. She has forgotten. I guess there is always tonight when she gets home from work to give her a kiss and hug. I'm going to remind her that she forgot this morning, though. I lay in bed for a while until my alarm tells me it's time to get up. I wait another five minutes and then push myself out of bed. I notice that the ring that I had bought the day before at the craft fair is missing. Darn! I really wanted to wear it to school today. I search my bed to no avail. If I waste any more time, I will be late for the bus and then Carl, my stepdad, will be mad at me and then I would have to ask him for a ride to school. He already thinks I mess everything up; I don't want to give him another excuse not to like me. Sometimes I feel like he is just waiting for another reason to send me away again.

I abandon my search and decide to wear the ring my mom gave me four years ago for my seventh birthday, before she met Carl. My eleven-year-old finger is getting too big for it now, so I don't wear it often. It is made of silver, very tiny and delicate, in the shape of a butterfly to match the birthmark on my right forearm that's almost level with my elbow on the inside of my arm. The ring also has a teeny tiny diamond in the center of the butterfly. I try to slip it on, but it feels tight on the finger I used to wear it on, so I try it on my pinkie and it feels better. I finish dressing. I decide to wear my pink stretch pants and my favorite kitty shirt. It looks cold outside, so I throw on my pink windbreaker. Then I go across the hall to peek in to my baby sister's room. Last night my mom was folding laundry in the baby's room and I was sort of helping as I laid on the bed. I used the time to try to convince my mom how much I needed a dog; I guess I was a little annoying. Because she just kept repeating the word "No" over and over again. It's just I really, really want my own dog. There are puppies down the street from us, and every chance I get I go down there and pet them through the fence. I don't know why I can't have one. The other day I had to write a paper in school about "If I had one wish." I wished for my own dog. I would name it Buddy, and he would follow me everywhere and do tricks and love me the most. I really hope my mom will let me have a dog one day.

I showed my eighteen-month-old sister a new trick last night, too. I showed her how to jump up and down in her crib really high. It made her laugh so hard. I love making her laugh. She is almost ready to start climbing out of her crib, I think. I peek in and I see she is still sleeping, so I creep out quietly.

I feel a little queasy this morning and briefly consider telling Carl, my stepdad, that I feel sick and can't go to school today but change my mind to avoid an argument. The truth is I really don't want to stay home all day with him anyway. I look forward to going to school most days because it gives me time away from all of his criticism. Maybe eating some breakfast will make my tummy feel better. I go to the kitchen to make my lunch and breakfast. I decide on instant oatmeal, peaches and cream flavor. The microwave clock reads 6:30. I know I must start up the hill soon in order to catch the bus. I eat my oatmeal quickly. I'm glad Carl isn't in here watching me scarf down my oatmeal. He already thinks my table manners are atrocious and takes every opportunity to let me know what he thinks.

One time he didn't like the way I was eating my dinner, so he made me go sit in the bathroom in front of the mirror and watch myself eat. I don't think I'd ever make my kid do that if it was me. I just don't understand why he doesn't like me. I make a PB&J for my lunch, throw in an apple and juice box, and check one more time to see if Shayna is awake yet, but she is not, so I must leave without telling her good-bye. I haven't seen Carl all morning. I think he must be outside because he is not inside like he usually is, watching TV. I see my cat, Monkey, outside on the deck. My grandma Ninny gave him to me before we left for Tahoe. Monkey is a black Manx, which means he has no tail.

When we got him I wanted to name him Sapphire because he had the bluest eyes, but Carl thought it was a stupid name and just started to call him Monkey. At first it really made me mad, and I called him Sapphire every chance I got, but as Monkey has grown, the name Sapphire really doesn't suit him, and now I call him Monkey, too. It's funny how you can get used to things. Monkey mostly stays outside, but I let him in at night and he sleeps with me. I don't like to leave him outside at night because my mom's cat Bridget was eaten by a wild animal after we moved up here to Tahoe. It was awful; we had been looking for her for days and I finally found what was left of her, which was nothing more than a pile of fur. It was really sad. Monkey must have been separated from his mom at a young age because he loves to nurse on my fuzzy blanket. I think he thinks I'm his mom.

Me, Monkey, and Bugsy

I go outside on the deck and give him a pet hello, he meows for food, so I give him a little handful of cat food. I have also brought out a carrot for Bugsy, the black-and-white dwarf rabbit that's not so little. Carl had Bugsy when I met him a few years ago. I think the cutest thing about Bugsy is his love of grape-flavored popsicles. It is my job to clean his cage, which is not my favorite thing to do. He really poops a lot. I read in a book once that rabbits eat one poop a night. It's funny how sometimes animals do things that don't make sense to people, but I think they must have a good reason for doing it; I just can't figure out what that may be.

Tahoe house in winter

I make my way out the front door, down the long walkway to the stairs. Our house in Tahoe reminds me of a ski cabin. It is located at the bottom of a hill. We have lived here since September of last year. We used to live in Orange County. We had a break-in at the apartment we were living in and my mom and Carl thought it would be safer if we moved to Tahoe. We live in a much smaller town now.

I grew up in Anaheim, California. I've always thought that when we moved in with Carl, he convinced my mom that it was time that I started walking to school by myself because I had never done it before. I don't think my mom liked the idea very much, but she couldn't be there to drive me in the morning because she had to go to work early, so that left Carl to take me and sometimes he would and sometimes he wouldn't be there, so I had to walk. They gave me a key to the apartment we lived in at the time, and that was the first year I walked home from school by myself.

One time as I was walking home from Lampson Elementary where I went to fourth grade, a car with a group of guys in it started shouting at me and gesturing for me to come over. I started running and hid in a bush until the car passed, then I ran home as fast as I could and locked the door behind me. I was scared to walk home after that and did it as fast as I could. Sometimes my mom or Carl would pick me up from school. I liked those days. Tahoe feels nothing like Anaheim. I can ride my bike anywhere and I don't feel afraid here.

There is a neighborhood dog named Ninja that comes over and walks up the hill with me some mornings. I want a dog of my own so badly, one that would walk up that hill with me every morning and then be there to greet me when I come home from school. Ninja the dog really prefers Carl over me, though, and usually only waits for him and goes on walks with him on the weekends.

This morning I was so hoping that Ninja would come and walk with me, but as I head out, there is no sign of her anywhere. As I leave the house for school, I yell to Carl that I am on my way up the hill. I don't see him or hear him answer, but see that he has his van out of the garage, so he must be working on it. I start out on the right side of the hill and then when it starts to curve, I switch to the other side. I have one more week of school left, then summer vacation starts. I have made plans with my friend Shawnee from school to work at a dude ranch. She loves horses and sometimes she draws them for me. I love the way she draws horses. She has taken me on a trail ride before and I loved it. She is a great rider. She used to live with her mother on a ranch, but now she lives a mile away from me in an apartment with her grandma Millie. I am so excited about our plans. I want to be as good a rider as she is one day. I still have to work up to asking Carl and my mom if I can do it. But I'm hoping it's something they will let me try. Carl is always saying I need to have more chores and that I need to learn more responsibility, so what better way for me to learn than to get a summer job? Well, at least that's how I'm going to present it to him and see what he says. Carl's sister, my new aunt M, has two horses. One is a girl and the other one is her baby foal. I love to go visit her. She is so nice to me compared to Carl and his mother W. M acts like she really likes me. She lets me sit with her on her horse and we walk around the arena. It's so much fun. She also has a really cute cocker spaniel, which loves to wrestle. I like visiting her; she seems to really like me.

When I lived in Orange County I was in a jazz class. I really didn't enjoy going that much. I really wanted to take ballet, but when my mom went to sign me up, the class for ballet was full and so we went for jazz. I'm really shy, and performing in front of people is not a strong suit with me. We moved to Tahoe right before my final recital. Thank goodness. I think I would have messed up if I had to perform in front of an audience. And wearing a leotard was not my cup of tea either.

When we moved to Tahoe after school started I joined a Girl Scout troop. Again, not my idea. It's hard to make friends, but some of the girls are also in my class, so that makes it easier. I just wish I wasn't so shy sometimes. I usually hang out with Shawnee, although she is not in my troop. But the girls are all nice and I like when we make things and sell cookies together. I am not good at going up to strangers' doors and asking them if they want to buy some Girl Scout cookies, but I am very good at eating Girl Scout cookies. My favorites are Samoas and Thin Mints. When it's my turn to go up to the door and sell, I knock on the door and let my partner do the talking. Will I ever get over my shyness? We have a class field trip to a water park coming up the last week of school. I want to go and have fun, but my body is changing and I'm self-conscious. I tried the other night to talk to my mom about shaving my armpits and my legs. I am embarrassed to be seen with all that hair. But I didn't know how to start that conversation. Need to think of something soon; the trip is only a few days away.

As I am walking up the hill to the school bus this chilly day in June, I am thinking how sometimes it feels like my life is dictated by something or someone else. For instance, when I play with my Barbies, I can plan out their lives and make them do all the things I want them to do. I feel sometimes that this is being done to me. I feel like my life is planned out for me, in what way

I do not know, but on this day I feel like a puppet on a string, and I have no idea who's on the other end.

I am coming to the part of the hill at which I have been taught to cross to the other side. Carl and my mom taught me this when we moved up here and it was decided that I would walk up to the bus stop to catch the bus for school. Carl said I should cross here so that oncoming traffic could see me and I could see what's coming at me, too. As I cross the road at the bend, I lose my train of thought and start to daydream about the summer. I walk in the gravelly part of the shoulder of the road. I haven't seen any cars go by at all this morning. There are bushes to my left. As I am walking, I hear a car behind me. I look back expecting the car to pass on the other side of the road going up, but to my surprise the car pulls up beside me. I was so lost in thought that the unusual behavior of the driver didn't register with me. I stop walking as the driver rolls down his window. He leans slightly out of his car and starts to ask me for directions. His hand shoots out of the window so fast I barely register that he has something black in his hand. I hear a crackling sound and I feel paralyzed. I take staggering steps back; fear erasing everything but the need to get away. As the car door opens, I fall to the ground and start to push back on my hands and butt toward the safety of the bushes. Scooting as fast as I can is my only goal—to make it to the bushes away from the man that is coming to grab me. My hand connects with something hard and sticky. What is it? It doesn't matter—I must hold on to it. Someone is dragging me and now I am being lifted. My limbs feel like they weigh a ton. I try to resist and try to push farther into the bushes. The paralyzing feeling returns accompanied by a strange electrical current zapping sound. I am helpless to resist for some reason. I don't understand why my body is not working. I realize I have peed my pants. Strangely I do not feel embarrassed. "No, no, no," I cry. My voice sounds harsh to my ears. The strange man hauls me up and shoves me into the backseat and down onto the floorboards of his car. My brain feels fuzzy. I don't understand what's happening. I want to go home. I want to crawl back into my bed. I want to play with my sister. I want my mommy. I want time to reverse itself and give me a do-over. A blanket is thrown on top of me and I feel a lot of weight on my back. I feel as if I can't breathe. I hear voices, but they are muffled. The car is moving. I want to get out of the car. I twist and turn, but something is pinning me down. I start to feel embarrassed about losing control of my bladder and want to get up and go home. I feel like I can't think right. I know what is happening to me is not right, but I don't know what to do. I feel scared and helpless. The car is moving and I feel sick. I need to throw up, but I'm afraid if I do I will choke to death, so I resist the feeling. Something tells me they wouldn't help me if I did. I am so hot. I feel as if my skin is burning. Please, please remove this hot blanket—I can't breathe! I feel like yelling, but my voice feels dry and nothing comes out. I lose consciousness. When I wake up, I hear voices. The car has stopped. Where are we? I hear two voices. One is male and the other is muffled and low, but it doesn't sound like a man's voice. The blanket is still covering me, but the weight has been taken off. I hear a car door open and slam shut very quickly. The blanket is finally pulled from my face and I can see the person that was in the backseat is now in the front, but I can't see a face; it's not someone big, so it could be a woman. I am offered a drink by the male that pulled me into the car. I am so hot and my mouth is so dry. He says he got an extra straw for me, so I don't need to worry about his germs. I am so grateful for that drink—my mouth feels so dry like I've been screaming for a long time, but I can't remember screaming at all. All of a sudden I hear him laugh. He is saying something about how he can't believe he got away with it. I want to tell him I want to go home. But I am so scared I am afraid to make the man angry. What should I do? I just don't know what to do. I wish I did. I'm so scared. I want to go to sleep and pretend this is not happening. Why is this happening? Who are these people and what do they want with me?

Reflection

Since my return back into the world, I find myself collecting pinecones. I ask the people I know now when they go on trips to bring me back a pinecone. I have pinecones from Lake Placid, Maine, and Oregon. My therapist and I finally solved my obsession. A pinecone was the last thing I touched before I was taken away by Phillip. A hard and sticky pinecone was my last grip on freedom before eighteen years in captivity.

Stolen

My head feels like it's spinning. I think I must have fallen asleep. When I come awake, we have stopped again. It is still daytime. The man tells the other passenger that we are home and then whispers something else that I can't hear. I still can't see the other passenger but can hear someone exit the car. The man that grabbed me tells me to be quiet and I won't be hurt. He says I need to be very quiet or I will upset his very aggressive dogs. I do not want to do anything to anger him or the dogs. He seems big to me. He says he is going to take me in the house and for me to be quiet and not say a word. He throws a blanket over my head and leads me somewhere. I want to go home. My brain feels less foggy than it did before. I tell myself I am having a dream and any minute I will wake up and my mom will be there to hold me and tell me it was all just a bad dream. But of course this is reality I must survive. I don't ever remember having a nightmare quite this vivid. I was afraid of ET for a while when I first saw the movie. I used to think that ET would come to my house and be all dressed up like when the little girl in the movie dressed him; in my dream, he was mad at me for that for some reason. That was a crazy dream but nothing as scary as this.

When we are inside the strange house, he takes off the blanket and instructs me to sit on the wicker sofa. He is a very tall man. He has very light blue eyes and brown hair that is thinning on the top a bit. His nose is kind of long and his skin is a bronze color. It looks like he spent too much time in the sun. He does not look like a bad guy. He looks like a normal guy. Like any ordinary guy you would see in everyday life. But he is not! He couldn't be . . . could he? He shows me a black thing with metal ends that look sharp. He calls it a "stun gun" and he says he will use it again if I try to get away. He turns it on and I hear the strange zapping sound I heard before when my body would not work. The sofa I'm sitting on has a lot of cat hair. I look up and I see a cat sitting on a washing machine. The cat looks like a Himalayan Persian tortoiseshell and there is another one that looks like a very fat, tabby torty. I ask if I can pet them. He says if they come to me, then I can. One comes over and I give it a pet. Its hair feels silky and real. I think this cat is the only thing that feels real right now; everything else feels like a nightmare but this is too real to be a dream. The man says to follow him.

Reflection

Looking back on that day, feelings of dread come to mind. I was eleven years old, still very much a kid. I was very scared and alone. I didn't know what was going to happen and if someone had told me what I would be enduring for the next eighteen years, I would never have believed them. I had no idea what was going to happen to me. What this man had in mind for me was like a foreign language. I had never been subjected to any form of sexual abuse before, hadn't ever heard the words either. My only reference to sex was what I had seen on TV or movies and then acted out when playing Barbies, which would be in the form of Barbie and Ken laying in the bed together side by side. That is what I thought "sex" was. I know—silly, right? But that is the truth. My aunt Tina says that I asked her once how babies were made and she explained it to me. I do not remember asking her this question and I don't remember her answer to me. Even if I had understood or remembered what she told me, it still would not have prepared me for what Phillip did to me. No amount of preparation could have helped me understand why another human being would do what he did to another human being, a little girl, for that matter. I still don't get it.

The Secret Backyard

I follow the man. I don't have a choice. There is nowhere to run. There is nowhere to hide. I have no idea where I am. Everything is turned upside down. All I can do is wait for my mom to come and find me. I wish I could be back at home right now. I would even like to hear a criticism from my stepdad Carl; anything familiar would be okay. Anywhere other than being here with this stranger that has hurt me with the stun gun. When we arrive at the bathroom in this stranger's house, he closes and locks the door. The shower is running and the strange man says that he wants me to take my clothes off. No, I say! Why does he want me to take my clothes off? I am very self-conscious of my body. The man says if I do not do it myself, he will do it for me. I am too scared to move, my body is shaking, so I do what is easy: I just stand there. He pulls down my pants and takes off my shirt. I am naked and very embarrassed. He stuffs all my clothes, shoes, and backpack in a bag.

He doesn't notice the tiny ring on my pinkie. I am relieved. I was afraid he would take that, too. He takes off his clothes and I try not to look. He asks if I have ever seen a naked man before and I answer no. He says that's hard to believe at my age. I have never seen a naked man before and know that I'm not supposed to look. The strange man tells me to look at him. I glance real quickly and want to start laughing in spite of my fearfulness. His private part looks so funny. In spite of myself, I smile, sometimes I laugh when I'm nervous; I don't mean to, it just comes out. The man says to touch it. It is small and squishy. The man says to make it grow. In my mind I think this man is crazy. This is the strangest weirdest man on the planet! I do not want to touch his private part, but the man insists, so I hold it in my hand. It is soft and paler than the skin around it. He says that's enough and tells me to get into the shower. I want to resist, but the man pushes me into the shower. He gets in the shower, too. He tells me to wash up and hands me the soap. I want to be asleep in my own bed not here in the shower with this strange man. I do as he tells me, not knowing what else to do. He then asks me if I have ever shaved my underarms and vagina. I say no, I haven't. I think to myself, this man wants me to do the exact thing that I have wanted to ask my mom if I can do, but why does he want me to do it in front of him? My upcoming field trip was going to be to a water park and I had been wanting to ask my mom if it was okay if I could shave my armpits and around my legs. I was embarrassed to be seen with all that hair, but I also didn't know how to ask my mom. The night before, I remember going to her bedroom wanting to ask her "the question." But instead I just sat there and never asked. I wonder what my mom would have said if I had asked her "the question" last night.

• • •

Now I am with this stranger who is asking me strange questions and all I can think about is my mom. My mom must be worried. Has anyone told my mom that I was taken by some stranger? How will she find me? The man shaves my armpits and legs and then he says he's going to shave my vagina hair. Why? I think to myself. When he's done, he says I can get out of the shower. I feel like I am in a nightmare that I have no control over. Silent tears start spilling over my cheeks. They feel hot against my cold skin. I start to shiver. I am so cold. I try to stop the tears. I tell myself I must be brave. It feels like my life is not my own anymore. My whole body feels heavy and I just want to collapse. This cannot be real, I tell myself. It's only a dream. I will soon wake up in my own bed. The man hands me a towel. I gladly wrap myself in it. It feels warm and safe. I want to bury my head in the towel. The feeling of safety the towel creates brings memories of when my mom would wrap me up after my baths—the floodgate in me opens and my silent tears become giant sobs. The man looks like he doesn't know how to respond; he tells me to calm down and be quiet, that he is not going to do anything more today. The man takes me in his arms and offers comfort. I do not want comfort from this awful man, but there is no one else here and I reluctantly lean into what comfort he gives. Up until now I have not cried one time. Only on the inside. Now I feel like a rabbit being comforted by a lion. I am so scared. My tears continue to run down my cheeks; I can feel them wet and warm. They once again become silent tears running down my face into nothingness. The man is saying things, but I'm not listening. The man speaks again in a louder voice, I become afraid because his voice is stronger; I make an effort to listen. He says he's going to take me somewhere else and that I must be very quiet or I will get in trouble; if I'm quiet and a good girl, everything will be fine. I ask him if I can put my clothes back on. He chuckles and says no. I ask him when I can go home. He says he doesn't know but he will work on it. I say my family doesn't have a lot of money, but they would pay a ransom to get me back. He looks at me and smiles and says, really? I said he just needs to let my mom know where I am. He just stares at me.

I walk in front of him down the small flight of stairs to the downstairs porch. Once again he puts the blanket on me. I have nothing on but the towel and the blanket now. My backpack is gone. My clothes are gone. My shoes are gone. All I have is the tiny butterfly ring on my pinkie that my mom gave me. I have nothing but this stranger and my feet to guide me. The first thing I feel is the hardness of concrete. Then my feet feel the tickling cold sensation of wet grass. I can't see my feet because he is holding me by my neck and my head can't go down. But I can feel the ground and I can hear a train. I think to myself I must remember that there is a train nearby so that when I am found I can tell whoever finds me that I was being held somewhere where I can hear a train. The next thing my feet feel are sticks or some kind of small branches and dirt. Some are pointy and sharp, and I can also feel rocks which hurt my feet. I try to tiptoe, but it's hard because he is leading the way and walks very rapidly. The rocks pass and now I feel we are back on hard cold concrete. I hear a gate or fence being pushed open and closed behind us. We walk a little further and I hear him fiddling with something that rattles and jingles. It sounds like a lock. I briefly wonder where the other person from the car is. I feel teeny tiny pebbles on my feet. He tells me to watch my step, that I need to step up to the step in front of me. I miss a little because I can't see it, but he has my arm, so I don't fall. I make the step up and feel hard carpet on the bottom of my feet now. Not the soft kind but the low-to-the-ground kind. I hear the door shut behind me. He leads me a little further into this new room. Then we enter another door. He takes the blanket off my head, and I see a bunch of blankets on the floor. Like what I used to sleep on when we moved into Carl's apartment. It only had one bedroom, so Carl said I could make a "pallet" in the living room. That's what he called putting an egg-crate mattress with blankets on the floor. This looks like that minus the egg-crate mattress. He says I can sleep there. All of a sudden I realize how tired I am. I feel like I can barely stand up. My whole body is shaking from head to toe. He says he will be back later and he wants me to stay in here and to be quiet. He says the door is locked and reminds me of the dogs outside that don't like trespassers and says to them I would be a trespasser. He says he has to put handcuffs on me, but that they have fur on them so they won't hurt too much. I shake my head no and say that I won't try to get away. He says he has to because he doesn't trust me yet. He says to put my hands behind my back. I continue to sit on the floor. He bends down and turns my body so he can put the cuffs on me. I can feel the cold metal and the soft fur. I don't like the way the cuffs feel heavy on my wrists. He helps me to lie down on my side. It is not comfortable to lay on your side with your hands behind your back. He says he will be back later to check on me and bring me something to eat. Then he is gone and I can hear the lock being put back on the door. The tears start again, softly at first then my silent sobs rack my body. I cry myself to sleep alone.

Reflection

To this day when I close my eyes and think back, I can still hear the sound of that lock. I can hear the squeak of the big, thick soundproof door closing me in. It gives me a strange feeling in the pit of my stomach when I think of the many long hours I spent in that room all alone.

Today I sometimes struggle with feelings of loneliness even when I am not alone. I think this feeling began in that room Phillip put me in. Hours turned into days, days to weeks, and weeks to months and then years. I have spent a lifetime alone, or so it seems to me sometimes.

I have gained a lot of freedom this past year. Being with my family and meeting new friends and reuniting with old has been a dream come true. People and animals keep the loneliness away. I know the feeling of loneliness is just in my head because I am not alone, but it still creeps back at times. I do enjoy time to myself. I love to read and write and spend time with my pets. I don't always mind the feeling of loneliness; it has given me the time to know who I am. However, my mind pulls me back to those days of confinement and I feel myself needing to call a friend or make a plan for lunch—anything to not be alone. I am working through these feelings. I enjoy life so much more now, and I try hard to appreciate each and every day, but deep down I am still afraid it will be taken away.

Alone in a Strange Place

When I wake I am alone in a strange place. I wonder how much time has passed. I woke up crying, which is strange because I've never had a dream scare me so much that I've woken up crying before. I realize that my nightmare is real. Why is this happening? My body feels tight and it hurts. My mind wants to leave and be somewhere else. I struggle to gain a sitting position, but the handcuffs make it difficult. I finally manage awkwardly. Maybe I should just try to go back to sleep. My mind is worrying about all the things I was supposed to do that day. What happened when I didn't show up at school? Will I get in trouble? Does anyone know what happened? Where is my mom? Is she still at work? Is she looking for me? Did Carl see this man take me? Is he sending someone to get me? When can I go home? Will this stranger take me home? All these questions go through my mind. My head still feels fuzzy. I don't know what to do. I want to get up and see if the first door will open so I can see what's in the other room. But every time I try to sit up I fall back down. I am so tired. I turn so I am now lying on my back more, which is a little more comfortable. This room is small. My bed back at home would not fit in this room. There is a window above my makeshift bed. There is a towel and blinds covering the window, so I can only see a little bit of light. It looks like moonlight. I wish I could see the moon. My mom and I used to love to sit out front of my grandma's house and look at the moon. We would debate about which moon was better, the crescent or the full. I always voted for the full and she liked the crescent. I wonder what kind of moon is out tonight. It feels like I have been here forever. Has it been an hour or more? I have no way of telling. There are tall, heavy-looking tables in two corners of the tiny room I'm in. The legs are covered in carpet. There is also some strange-looking equipment on tables. I can't really see the tops because the handcuffs prevent me from getting up all the way. They are big and from what I can see from this angle have sliding dials on them. There is also a big pane of glass in the wall that separates this room from the next. The walls are made of some kind of wood. It looks like a lot of different woods all mixed together to create a panel that has many colors. I think it is called particleboard, but I'm not sure. I want to feel it but instead scrape my knuckle along the side of it. It is very rough and I think I got a splinter in my knuckle. I wonder what will happen to me. I can't get comfortable. I move from side to side. I want to get up and walk around. My legs feel like they are falling asleep and are getting cramps. I lay back down and fall asleep quickly.

The towel on the window shows that the sun is up. This room is getting hot when I wake the next morning; at least I think it is morning. There is really no way to know for sure. I feel like I can't breathe, it's so hot. I am so thirsty and I'm starting to sweat. How much time has passed? I close my eyes thinking, Will I ever want to open them again? Maybe if I go to sleep, then when I wake up I will be in my own bed and this will be just a bad dream. I close my eyes and give in to oblivion once again.

Reflection

He did come in that day to check on me. He brought me fast food and a soda. It's hard to remember day-to-day things after this point. I think he came in at least once a day to bring me something to drink and eat. I became totally dependent on him for everything. He would take off the handcuffs while he was there so I could eat. He brought in a bucket for me to use as a toilet. I hated when he would put the cuffs back on when he left, so eventually I looked forward to seeing him and getting them off. Even though they were covered in soft fur, they still bit into my wrists and made my skin raw. It was hot in that room and I would sweat buckets all day. He said he was working on getting a cooler for the room and that would make it cooler for me. In the meantime he brought in a fan, which helped a lot. I would ask him every day when he was going to let me go home. I guess I can kind of figure out the answer to that even if I don't remember his exact words.

He would try to make me smile with all these silly voices he would make. He had an English accent, a Texan accent, and an Australian accent. I feel this was all part of his plan to manipulate me into being compliant with him. He used his powers of persuasion to gain my trust. He became my entire world. I depended on him for food, water, my toilet. He was my only source of amusement. I craved human contact so much by then that I actually looked forward to him coming to see me; it felt like he was bestowing a gift to me . . . his presence. He was all I knew for months. I slept a lot during this time. There was nothing else to do and sleeping helped to shut off my broken heart. I didn't have any more nightmares like that first one about being taken; I guess I was living the ultimate nightmare so my mind couldn't think of anything worse. When I dreamed, I dreamed I could fly. When I would wake, I would have no concept of time. A little light leaked through the towel on the window, but other than that not much light. I learned to gauge the time by Phillip's visits. I knew it must be night when Phillip would bring my dinner. He didn't touch me after that first day in the bathroom until one day about a week later . . .

The First Time

I hear the lock rattle and know he is coming to feed me. I am very hungry today. I can't remember the last time I ate. I'm not sure how long I have been in this room. I tell myself I should start counting days because when I am rescued I will need to be able to know how long I have been in this room. I have no way of keeping track of the days. The handcuffs are making my wrists raw and make it hard to use my hands. I have nothing to write on or with. He always brings me a soda, so I think maybe if I can save the paper on the straw, then I can count the days by how many straw papers I have, but he always takes the trash from me and puts on the cuffs and there is no time for paper straw saving. I try to keep track of the days by how many times the sun sets, but I fall asleep so easily and sometimes when I wake it is dark already. I can see a little light coming through the window but not much. It is either very early or the sun is setting. When the sun is up and the wind blows, the shadow on the towel that is hanging over the window looks like a person hanging from it. I have nicknamed this tree "hangman's tree." One time curiosity got the better of me and I struggled to get up with the handcuffs and finally got to my feet. I wanted to see what was hanging outside the window. I grabbed a corner of towel with my teeth and wiggled and maneuvered until I could see out of the window as best I could. There was nothing but a medium-sized tree outside the window, nothing hanging from it but its large gangly branches and thick, full-size leaves. I am relieved to see just the tree; I don't know if I can stand any more strangeness.

It's a very strange feeling to not go to school every day. I sometimes miss the routine I used to have, and sometimes it's nice to not have to get up and go to school, too. But I am so bored. There is nothing to do in this place. I make up stories in my head a lot. I have made up one about a boy that has come from the stars. He flies around the world and when he hears a child crying he always come to investigate. I imagine that one day this Star Boy hears me crying because I cry every single day. He thinks my cries are especially heart wrenching, and so he combs the earth in search of me. When he finds me he is able to open the window of my prison and I take his hand and he flies me all around the world. But in the end he always returns me to my prison. I wonder why this is so.

I can hear my captor's hollow footsteps coming from the room beyond. He enters the door and has a milkshake in his hand. At first I smile at him and want him to think I am doing well. For some reason I think it is important for me to be happy around him. He comes in and crouches down and he says today will be a little different. He says I can have the milkshake and something to eat after we are done. Done with what? All of a sudden I am not hungry anymore. I have this terrible feeling in the pit of my stomach. I want him to go away. I want to go away. I tell him I am not hungry. I just want to go home. He puts the milkshake on a shelf and bends down. He says to take off my towel and lay back on the pallet. He takes off the cuffs and re-locks them in front of me instead of behind my back. He then sits down next to me and explains what he is going to do. He stands back up and takes off all his clothes. I do not want him to do that. I start to cry. He takes my handcuffed hands and holds them over my head. I feel so helpless and vulnerable. I feel so alone. He lies on top of me. He is so heavy. I can't stop crying. He said he'd be quick and it would be better if I didn't struggle because then he wouldn't have to get aggressive. I don't under-stand any of this. He forces my legs open and inserts the hard thing between his legs in me. It feels like I am being stretched apart. I feel like it's going to come out of my belly. I am so small and he is so big. Why is he doing this? Is this normal? I try to scoot away. I try to close my legs. He just takes hold of my legs and shoves them further apart. He is too heavy and strong for me. He keeps my hands above my head. I try to think of anything but what is happening to me. Look anywhere except his face. I can feel the tears on my cheeks. He is making strange noises and grunting and sweating all over me. I can't breathe he is so heavy. All of a sudden he makes a giant grunt and puts even more of his weight on me as he collapses. I cannot do anything. I cannot move. He finally moves and asks if I'm okay. He says it would be easier on me if I didn't resist or struggle so much next time. He says it wouldn't hurt as much. I think to myself, If you didn't do it in the first place then it wouldn't hurt at all. But I am too frightened by his act to say a thing in objection to him. In my mind I am screaming NO I AM NOT OKAY . . . GET OFF OF ME! Why are you doing this? What does it mean? He said it was all over now and he gets up and says he's going to go get something to clean me up. I am bleeding "down there." I am so scared. Am I dying? Why am I bleeding? He says it's okay—he just "popped my cherry." I don't know what he meant. He leaves and comes back with a bucket of warm water and a washcloth. He takes the cuffs off and says he will go into the next room and give me some privacy to bathe. I wash up and wrap myself in the clean towel and then sit back down on the pallet on the floor. Milkshake all but forgotten.

Reflection

I had to stay in the same place I'd just been raped in. I didn't know at the time that is what it was called; the word "rape" was not in my vocabulary. Today that makes me feel terrible for that little naïve girl. She is still a part of me and at times she comes out and makes me feel small and helpless once again. At times I feel like I'm still eleven years old. But something inside that frightened little girl made her a survivor and she has made me the person I am today. That rape turned out to be the first of many frequent encounters. I don't remember if he came in every day to have sex with me; all I know is it happened more times than I can count. Each time it happened I learned to "go away" in my mind until he was finished. I would make up stories in my head to pass the time. It was easy for me in those early days to escape into my dreamworld because I had always been a dreamer and had my head in the clouds a lot. I used to lose all track of time and it helped to keep me from going crazy.

Knowing my kidnapper's name was not something I wanted to know. I remember thinking that I did not want know his name because I had heard that once you know their name, they can never let you go. During the first week or so I did learn that my kidnapper's first name was Phillip. I don't remember how I knew; it wasn't like he introduced himself. He revealed it subtly without me realizing it.

I can't believe how much I came to rely on him for everything. I remember the heat was getting really bad and I was so thankful to him when he finally installed an air-conditioning unit. It seemed he had an answer for everything. Phillip seemed like a nice guy when he wasn't using me for sex. I even started enjoying his company. I was naïve and desperately lonely. I was locked in a room all by myself for days on end, and he was my only contact with the outside world. All I could do was survive and endure . . .

Hours later as I lay staring at the ceiling, I notice the forgotten milkshake has enticed the ants to come. I regret not drinking it because now I am so hungry my stomach is growling at me. There is a long trail of ants that leads from the window to the milkshake. Some have ventured further and now I think they are starting to explore me. Maybe I smell so bad it is attracting them. I don't know how long it's been since I had a shower. I haven't had one since that first day when he had me get in the shower with him. Since then, the only cleanup I've had is with a bucket of water. The ants make my skin itch even worse than my unclean body already does and sometimes they get in my mouth and leave a spicy flavor behind. The cuffs make it near impossible to scratch and flick them away. I wish I could get in a nice hot bath and just soak all the grime away.

First Kitty

He says he is going to get me a kitty. I have been telling him how lonely I am and how much I love cats and all about the ones I used to have. I am so excited I can't wait to have a kitty to talk to. All I do is lie here in this room all day long. I am so bored. He doesn't leave the cuffs on me anymore. One day after he was done having sex with me, he said if I promised to be good he would leave the cuffs off. He was going to trust me because he didn't want to put them back on me; he wanted me to be more comfortable. I thought of many things I could say, but none of them were polite, so I just nodded. After he left and I got cleaned up in the bucket of water he left, I thought about venturing into the other room that is attached to the room that I am in. I made sure that I could hear the lock on the outer door click closed before I even dared to move, then I sat up and listened to all the sounds I could hear. Sometimes I can hear him coming even before I hear the lock. I can hear a lot of things that I never noticed before. I listen to the outside a lot. I hear the train—the whistle and how it rolls on the tracks. I can hear someone mowing the grass. I can hear birds. And I can hear airplanes overhead. I miss being outside. I am so bored just sitting in here. I even miss brushing my teeth. Oh, what I would give for a toothbrush! I will never forget the time my stepfather Carl grounded me for not brushing my teeth. He believed in brushing after every meal. I admit I sometimes didn't brush after every meal. One day my friend Shawnee must have called and he picked up the phone without telling me. She asked him if she and her dad could take me with them to the movies. I guess he said yes, and a little while later she was knocking on the front door. I answered the door and was surprised to see her because I didn't know she was coming; Carl didn't tell me. She asked if I was ready to go to the movies; she assumed Carl had told me about the movie and that I should get ready. Carl announced I couldn't go because I didn't brush my teeth after breakfast. He said he had checked and the brush was dry. I pleaded with him. I said I would go brush them right now, I said I brushed them when I woke up, I added I really wanted to go and if I had known I would have brushed my teeth. But he refused to relent, and I stayed behind with tears running down my face as Shawnee and her dad went off to the movies together. For some reason that day sticks in my head. I'm thinking about it because I don't have a toothbrush and I know Carl would be really mad at me given that I haven't brushed my teeth in weeks. It would be funny to see the look on his face if I ever told him that. I do try to keep my teeth clean by using my finger to scrape off the plaque. It's amazing how much plaque actually builds up on teeth, especially the back ones. My tongue works for polishing, too. I wonder if I will ever be given a toothbrush again.

I sleep a lot to pass the time. If I ever get to go home again, the first thing I want to do is hug my mom and never let go. The second thing I can't wait for is to run free. My legs are so cramped here. I miss being able to run outside with my friends. If I ever get to go home, I would love to have my own dog. If I ever get the chance, I will run along the beach with my faithful dog by my side. I will take my dog everywhere with me and never be alone again. We will take long hikes together and he will run by my side as I ride my bike.

I finally rally my courage and decide to check out the other room. I am very curious to see what's in there. As I creep in, it is very dark. There are no windows that I can see. There is a drum set and microphone stands and big huge speakers throughout the room. Phillip told me that he used to play music in here before I came. Sometimes Phillip brings his guitar in and plays music and sings to me. Sometimes I feel like I've heard his songs before. Once I asked and he said he wrote all the songs himself. He thinks he's going to have a big music career one day. I wonder. He says he is very good. And someday he will be famous. I know I'm not supposed to, but I try to push on the big door that leads to the outside. It is solidly locked. There is no hope of escaping. I don't know what I would have done if it had actually opened. I have no idea where I am, and Phillip says that the Dobermans are still patrolling the yard. I fear he will find out that I tried to open the door somehow. He seems to know everything. I don't want to get in trouble. I just want to go home.

I tiptoe very quietly back to my room and look around. I check out the strange equipment now that I can get a close-up view of them. I asked Phillip what they were and he said they were mixers for mixing his music. He said they cost thousands of dollars, but his mother, Pat, bought them for him for his music career. He said he can mix his own music and he didn't need someone else to do it for him. That way it could be just the way he wanted it to sound. I had never heard of a mixer before.

Before he left today he brought me a very small black-and-white TV. It doesn't get many channels, but at least I can hear people talking. At night it gets much better reception and I watch the late shows. During the day it only gets infomercials and QVC. Very boring, but I seem to like it more and more. Sometimes like today I fall asleep to the sound of some lady trying to sell me an opal necklace.

I wake up the next morning . . . at least I think it is still morning. I think I am getting more used to sensing what time it is. Phillip usually comes to see me in the morning and then again during the evening when it gets dark. I'm hoping he will bring me my new kitty today.

I feel like I haven't eaten for a while. I can finally go to the bathroom anytime I need to. He has left a bucket for me in the corner covered with a piece of wood. I feel better knowing I don't have to hold it in until he comes. I sometimes look out the window. I have seen the dogs he talks about. Other than that, all I see are fences and weeds. I wonder if there are any people nearby. I wonder where I am.

I can hear him unlocking the door. He is coming. Now I can hear his footsteps. I hope he hasn't come for sex. He walks in and tells me to close my eyes. He says he has a surprise for me. I close my eyes and when I open them I see my new kitty. It looks like it is a couple months old and looks half-grown already. I feel disappointed. I was hoping for a little kitten, but I do not want him to see that I am disappointed. I smile and act happy. I am happy I will have company. The kitty meows and he hands it to me. I ask if it's a boy or girl, and he says it's a girl. She looks kind of like a dark tiger. With stripes running down her back. I pet her, and he says he is going to go find a box for the litter. I try to think of a name for her and I decide on Tigger—bouncing Tigger from *Winnie the Pooh*. Tigger is always happy and never sad. My new Tigger starts to explore her surroundings, and I sit back and watch her. Phillip comes back with a litter box and food and water. Then he says that he has to go and take Nancy to work. I have asked him about the other person that was with him when he got me, and he says that it was Nancy, his wife. At first he wouldn't tell me and would just say it was just some person that wasn't around anymore, but sometimes I can hear him talking to someone outside, and I kept wondering who that was and he finally told me. I wonder if I will get to meet his wife, Nancy. I hope so. I would really like to meet her. I am so lonely. Maybe one day she will come in and talk to me.

I have plans to teach my new kitty to come when I call her. I can't wait to get started. He leaves and says he will be back later. Again, I hope it's not for sex. Sometimes if I think really hard on something that I don't want to happen, it doesn't happen. It's the stuff that I don't think about that happens. So I try to think of everything that he could possibly do so it doesn't happen. This is my theory, but it doesn't always work because he always comes back for the sex. He says I am helping him with his sex problem. He says that instead of him hurting other people with his "problem," he took me and brought me here so I could help him and he wouldn't have to hurt anyone else ever again. I think that sounds really weird, but I also don't want him to do what he is doing to me to someone else. So what choice do I have? I'm hoping if he sees that I am good and does what he says that he will let me go home soon. When he is not hurting me, he likes to make me laugh. He says he likes it when I smile. Right now it is hard to find a reason to smile, but I think it best to keep him happy.

I think I have missed the field trip to the water park by now. I wonder if it was fun. I wonder what Shawnee is doing right now. I miss playing with her. And I was going to send my best friend Jessie a letter soon. I miss her so much. Ever since I moved to Tahoe I never get to see her anymore and I miss playing with her. I wonder if I will ever see her again. I wonder if anyone is looking for me. I can't remember a day since "the day" that I haven't cried. Will I ever again have a day without crying? I wonder what my mom is doing right now.

He is coming to take my Tigger away. I am so sad. He says he can't stand the smell when he comes in and the cat is peeing everywhere in here. I want to deny everything he says, but I can't. I don't think this is a good environment for Tigger. She wants to get out and run and play. She is tired of being in this room. I think that's why she is acting out and peeing everywhere. I have begun to feel guilty for asking for her in the first place. I should have thought about the place we were going to put her. This is no place for a kitty. He says his aunt is an animal lover and will take her. I am happy she will go to a happier place. But I am still sad. I will be alone again. The time has come and he takes her away. He says that maybe one day I can see her again and I shouldn't cry about it.

Reflection

It hurts to write about this part. This has turned out to be a very hard book to write. Part of me does not want to continue. To reenter the state of mind I was at that age is difficult and twists my insides. The more I write, the harder it becomes. On the one hand, I want to go on. I feel that if I don't, then I continue to protect my kidnapper and rapist and I don't have the need to do that any longer. On the other hand, this is something I have worked hard to put behind me and to write about it in such detail years later is difficult. To get inside my head and relive all this stuff that happened back then is terribly hard for me . . . I want to go on and I will finish it . . .

Father's Day, 2010

Yesterday was Father's Day and the man that I have been told is my father issued a statement in essence telling me to call him. He's saying he's dying of cancer. I did not call. I feel torn. I do not know this man that is my father. I do not want to feel sorry for this man that has chosen not to be a part of my life.

When I was nine, I became curious as to who my dad was. I would wonder if maybe he was a prince. That would explain why he couldn't live with us because of his many duties to his country, or maybe he was a navy ship captain that died on a secret mission. I wondered if he loved me. I guess around the time my sister was born, I started to notice other kids around me with dads and then there was my little sister with a dad that doted on her, and I wanted one, too. I noticed my stepfather, Carl, treated my sister so differently than he had been treating me. It made me feel unloved and unwanted.

I remember asking my mom what my real dad's name was and she replied, "His name is Ken." And I remember smiling and said, "Like Barbie's Ken?" I asked if she had a picture, but she didn't. I asked if he had ever seen me, and she said that he had chosen not to. I didn't understand why at the time. But it made me feel sad. After that I didn't bring up the subject again. I had my mom, who I knew wanted me and loved me, and I wanted that to be enough.

The next time I remember thinking about the man that fathered me was when I was kidnapped. For a brief second I thought maybe this was my father who took me. I know now this was the farthest thing from the truth. I even asked Phillip if he was my father in the beginning and he immediately said no.

Now as I sit and write about these moments of my life, I feel confused. What should I feel? What should I think? I must answer these questions on my own now. For so long decisions were made for me. This confusing topic was not something I had to think about in that backyard.

I don't want to have to make a decision on this issue right now. I want time to adjust and make a life for myself and my family before I decide whether or not I want a relationship with my biological father. I am still coming to terms with the manipulation I suffered at the hands of Phillip. I don't need another man issuing me ultimatums. I know what I want. I want more time to decide. I want to be in charge of when I feel I'm ready to meet this stranger and his family. Even though it has been almost a year from my captivity, I don't feel the time is right. I am through with living with other people's demands and wants. I feel guilt where there should be no guilt. It was not me who chose not to see his daughter when he had the chance. He could have made the effort to come and visit for the first eleven years of my life. He made the choice not to. He made that choice, and I am not condemning him for it. But by choosing to not be a part of my life back then; now I am an adult and I get to choose if and when I want to see him.

I have not had many positive male role models in my life. Since my release I have been introduced to some amazing fathers. I finally see with my own eyes what a father truly is and what it means to each of them. I see what good men are supposed to act like. Although each father is unique in his own way, they all have one thing in common—genuine love for their children. I met a dad that has part-time custody of his son. Although he does not see his son 24/7, their bond is deep and binding. You can see it by the way they interact and talk to each other. He never claims to be the perfect dad, but he strives to be better than the dad he had. He wants to be in his son's life through good times and bad. In my mind this makes him a super dad. He reminds me of my mom in a lot of ways. Another dad I have met is a stepfather. My experience with stepfathers wasn't the greatest. In my mind a stepparent never loves the stepkid as much as their own. I guess I think this way because I never felt loved or accepted by my stepfather. Now I see there are many forms of love and a stepparent can love their kids and the stepkids differently but still love and accept them. Although some stepparents and stepkids might not see eye-to-eye on some things, they can still have genuine affection for one another. I have never seen this stepfather making fun of his stepkids like Carl used to do to me. Shayna was his daughter; there was no doubt about that. He was very proud to have a daughter of his own. It left me feeling in the way. Perhaps this added to my sense of loneliness that I feel I have carried around for a long time.

I don't know why my biological father made the choice not to see me. I might never know the answer. I know now that he has two families, and I wonder if he takes the time to appreciate them. I know he must feel badly about what happened to me, but it was not his fault and could not have been prevented. Well, maybe it could have been prevented by some law changes and more supervision for sex offenders by the government, but that's hindsight. No one could have foreseen what would happen to me or ever thought it was possible in that small Tahoe community. The fact is it happened. It's over now. I do not live my life constantly wishing that I could change the past. I am thankful to be alive. I am thankful for my daughters. I am thankful I have an incredibly strong mom who never gave up on me. I am thankful for my beautiful, bright sister and loving aunt. And I am thankful for the countless others I have come to know since my rescue. Genes, I have learned, do not make a family. Families are the people that stick around through good and bad times. Sadness is part of life. Choosing to be happy and see the glass half full is a struggle we all must make. At this point I don't know what the future holds for me. I am enjoying what freedom I have and discovering things about myself I never knew. Will I choose to meet my biological father one day? I don't know the answer to that. I know for now I am not ready, and if that's too hard for him to understand, then that's too bad for him because I think I just might be worth waiting for.

The First "Run"

I just want to sleep. I sleep a lot, because when I sleep I can dream about better things, like being home with my mom and sister. When I wake it is dark, but something has woken me up. I hear the rattle of the lock. He is coming. He usually doesn't come this late. I have not thought he would come this late. I should have thought of all the possibilities and this wouldn't have happened. I am scared. What does he want? I want to sleep. He enters with a flashlight. I pretend to be sleeping. I squeeze my eyes tight. How long can I pretend to be asleep? I can hear him crouching down in front of me. Go away, I scream in my head. He shakes my shoulder and I pretend to wake up. He whispers to me, "It's time to wake up, we are going next door," and puts the blanket on me.

A few days ago, he brought in a pink flowered one-piece jumpsuit for me to wear and a pair of undies. It feels good to have something to wear. I hate taking it off when he comes for sex. Where are we going? This is different, I haven't left this building since I got here. He says I need to be quiet as we make our way out of the building. I cannot see where he is leading me, but we are there quickly, so it must not be far away. I have taken about ten steps when we arrive "next door."

We have entered another room. This one is different. It's all one room with three windows. Two of the windows are on each side of the building and the third one is by the door. On the back wall halfway up is a cooler unit in the wall, but there are no windows on that wall. I see that there are iron bars on these windows, too, before he moves to cover them with towels. He is using a flashlight and doesn't turn on the lights until he has locked the doors. There are two doors back-to-back—one on the outside with heavy iron bars and the inner wooden door can be locked from the inside. I am standing frozen with fear and shaking from head to toe. The unknown is the scariest thing for me and I have no idea what to expect. I feel so alone I even long to go back to my little room next door. At least I know what to expect over there. I look around the room. I glance at the three windows he has now covered with towels and think, No one to save me from this, nowhere to go.

There is a blue couch in the center of the room; it separates the room into two halves. A partition separates the back of the couch with a desk on the other side. The desk has lots of junk on it. As I look at the door, to the right is a little refrigerator that sits on a wooden cabinet with storage underneath. To the left of the door there is a toilet with a built-in bucket. As I turn around I see beyond the couch a TV on a stand. I notice a black trash bag sitting by the couch. There is also a stool under the window.

Reflection

I just noticed I was trying to distract myself from writing this part. I saw a spot on my computer and for some reason it was very important to get that spot off right now even though I know it's been there for months. My mind knows that what comes next is not easy for me. I am finding ways to avoid it. Avoiding things has worked to my advantage in the past. At other times, like now, it is just an inconvenience. I want to not be afraid of letting people know what really happened to me all those long years ago.

When I was first found I was adamant that there would be no book, no one would ever know what happened. In the months that have followed I feel I have grown so much. With the help of my mom and my family and especially my therapist I have come to realize that I can now do things for myself. I can make my own decisions and not worry about it if it's not what someone else wants. But most of all I have come to realize that I no longer need to protect him, Phillip Garrido. He no longer, or ever really, needed or deserved my protection. It has taken time for the guilt to wear off. But after living with him for so long I am amazed at how good I feel that I am no longer subject to him.

It is incredible, the depth of his manipulation. It did not feel like manipulation at the time. Only distance and time have revealed what life was like there and what life looks like from the outside. While I was there I would tell myself it could be worse; there are so many people in the world in worse situations than mine. At least I had a place to live. But what kind of life did I have really? No house. No real family. No friends. No, life was not what it should have been. My life depended on Phillip Garrido.

In my heart I do not hate Phillip. I don't believe in hate. To me it wastes too much time. People who hate waste so much of their life hating that they miss out on all the other stuff out here. I do not choose to live my life that way. What is done is done. I'm looking to the future. For the first time in a long time I get to look to the future instead of just the present. I have lived one day to the next never daring to look ahead. I never knew what was going to happen. If all my heart was filled up with hate and regrets and what ifs, then what else would it have room for? I won't say every day has been glorious and wonderful, but even on the bad days I can still say one thing—I am free . . . free to be the person I want to be . . . free to say I have my family and now new friends . . . I have nothing to feel ashamed about. I am strong and want to continue writing my story . . .

And then I see it. In the corner by the desk there is a bucket of water. Oh no! I think to myself I don't want to . . . No! . . . No! But what can I really do? Nothing. There is no one here but me and him. The door is locked. I want to cry. But I don't. He is talking now. He talks a lot, I notice, but doesn't really say important things. He just likes to hear himself talk, I think. It's easier to just agree with him because if you don't he'll explain it in detail and go on forever. He says something about going on a "run." I doubt if he means he's going outside for a real run; it's late and dark outside. He explains to me that a "run" is something he is going to be doing periodically and that I will be staying up with him for a few days depending on how much crank he is going to take. He says that crank is a drug that lets him stay up for longer periods of time. He says he really amazes himself by how much crank he can smoke or snort at one time. He says he can take hit after hit and it doesn't hit him as hard as a regular person. He says he has out-smoked his friends before and he has a high tolerance to all forms of drugs. He says he is explaining all this to me so I know what's going on and I will know what is expected of me. He says the "run," as he calls staying up for days, will be a time for him to fulfill all his fantasies and I will help him do that. He says the crank allows him to focus on one thing for a long time. He says first he's going to get me dressed the way he wants and then depending on his mood, the rest will consist of me masturbating him, sucking his penis, me in whatever position he desires, and dancing over him while he masturbates. He says for me to start by getting cleaned up with the bucket of water in the corner. He wants me to shave my vagina because he doesn't like hair because it gives him a rash. After that he is going to dress me and then I can put on some makeup. Makeup? Why does he want me to put on makeup? Why do I have to do any of this? It's stupid and I hate it. I don't want to do what he wants. I don't want to take off my clothes. I don't want to do any of it. I just want to go home! I think to myself. On the outside all I let go is a few tears. I'm afraid he will see me crying and become angry. He has already told me not to cry because it will interfere with his fantasy. I'm trying so hard not to cry.

He sees me hesitating and picks up the stun gun, I go over to the bucket and clean myself a little, when I am done he drags over the bag of clothes and starts to dress me in tight clothes. He makes holes in weird places.

I have been standing for what feels like hours now. When will he get done? Do I want him to be done? What's going to happen next? I guess he finally is happy with his creation. He tells me to lay on the bed in a certain way and then he gets undressed. He has a little bag of white powder. I'm not sure what it is. Maybe that's the crank he talked about. He shakes some out on the desk and uses a razor blade to chop it up a bit, then he puts it into a glass pipe and lights it and inhales from the other side. He asks if I want some and I say no. He says it helps him stay up, he calls it speed or crank. I think it is disgusting. I hate drugs. Is that why he is doing this—because of the drugs? He also rolls what he calls a joint and says its marijuana. He explains to me he has a sex problem and that he took me so I could help him with his problem so he wouldn't have to bother anyone else with his problem. He says it consumes his mind and that by me giving him an outlet I am saving others. Why me? Why can't he take care of his own problem? I don't want others to be hurt, though. Better me than someone else. The night seems endless and I am very tired. He has the lights on. All of them. It makes the room so hot. I have to touch his penis and stroke it up and down; he calls this "jacking off." Sometimes he wants me to suck on it, too. I hate it so much; it tastes disgusting. I am afraid the white stuff which he said is called cum will get in my mouth. I think this is really gross. He says the speed helps him to prolong the sex so he won't cum for a while. So I don't have to worry. This goes on and on for a while with him looking at these books he has. They look like photo albums, but they have kids from magazines cut out in different positions with penises taped on from other magazines. He looks at them and talks dirty to them, using words that are bad, some of which I have never heard before. He keeps doing the same thing over and over. When will this nightmare end? He also flips through the channels on the TV. He says he's looking for anything with a little girl with shorts on. I think it is finally morning now. The sun is coming through the windows that are covered with towels. I can see the sun through some of the cracks. He looks at the time and he says it's time to have sex. He tells me to lie down on my back. Part of me is relieved to get it over with. I was dreading it but want to go to sleep. I'm so tired. He gets on top of me and tells me he's going to talk really dirty to me and for me not to be scared. He says he's still the same person. He just needs to release the "monkey on his back." I can't help but cry, but they are silent tears. He fucks me as hard as he can it seems like. He uses that word a lot. My head is being pushed in between the couch and the pullout bed. I feel like I can't breathe. He is calling me a fucking whore and a cunt and other things. I want to be somewhere else, but I am here and I must not panic. It hurts more when I try to struggle, so I try not to get away from him, but it's hard not to want to push away from his sweaty disgusting body. Everything will be okay I tell myself. He will be the nice person soon. The one that likes to make me laugh and brings me good things to eat. I feel his release in me and finally it is over. He asks if I'm okay and I look at him and burst into tears. He takes me in his arms and says it's okay, that he is done, and that I can get cleaned up and go to sleep. He won't bother me like this for a while. I am so scared I don't know what to think. I want to believe him. He releases me to get up and put on his pants. He leaves to get me fresh water to bathe with. I am left alone. I hear the lock as it clicks. I wonder why he bothers. Where would I go? I don't know where I am. I feel so alone. Who would want me now? He comes back with the water and I get up, I am so sore. I am also bleeding again. He says it looks like I started my period. Tomorrow he will bring me some tampons and show me how to use them. For now he gives me some paper towels to stick in my underwear. I feel a little better now that I am dressed. He takes me back to the studio and says he will be back later with something really good to eat. He leaves and I am scared, tired and alone.

(The buildings that I write about are all in the part of the back-yard that Phillip made secret for eighteen years.)

Reflection

To see myself in that moment is very hard now. I was there and all this crap happened, but as I look back I can't help but look forward. I live in the present just as I always have and when I look back like this I see a very scared little girl just trying to survive. I wanted to go home to my mom more than anything, but I didn't know how. He said he took me so that he wouldn't have to hurt anyone else. In a way he made me feel special. I felt needed. Why I felt I needed that from this man I don't know. He would say terrible things like he would teach me how to be the best "sex slave" ever. And then there were other times that he was a very nice person. It confused me. When he would use bad language, it would scare me and make me feel horrible. One time he even threatened that he was going to sell me. This made me so scared. I didn't really know what it meant. When I asked why, he said I wasn't really doing the things that he wanted me to do. He said I cried too much and that it was hard for him to act out his fantasies when I was uncooperative and made him feel bad. I remember I begged him to please don't make me go with someone else, that I would try harder, and he could do anything he wanted and I would not fight. He said he would have to think about it. He said that these people that he was going to sell me to were planning to put me in a cage. It would be really bad for me. That it would be better for me if I stayed, but he didn't know if that was the thing for him to do. I remember shaking so hard on the couch. I didn't want to be put in a cage. He left me thinking that that was what was going to happen to me. When he returned that day and said we were going to go on a "run," I didn't dare ask if he had changed his mind. I

— 55 —

just tried to do everything just the way he told me. He never followed through on any of his promises. I will probably never forget feeling as afraid as I did that day. He never mentioned it again. Even when I went back to doing everything he wanted, I tried to rebel in my own little ways. Like sometimes I wouldn't put in as much effort as I could here and there. I wouldn't jack him off as fast as I could, forgetting (on purpose) to put lipstick on, and fake sleeping whenever he was engrossed in the TV. Little things that he wouldn't notice, but I still felt good inside for knowing I wasn't trying my best. I knew when to get serious, though, I was beginning to get a sense of his moods and when I could and when I could not mess around with him.

The "runs" were some of the most horrible moments of my life. I can't think of a good moment even when a "run" was over. I always knew there'd be a next time. I could see no end in sight. The horridness of being alone was always there, too. I really hated and despised it when he would leave me tied up in a certain position by those eye hooks that screw into the wall. He would screw them into the wall and then lift my legs with straps in different positions. One night he had been working on the position, trying to get it right for hours and realized he needed to go pick up Nancy from the nightshift where she worked a convalescent home. He said he was just going to leave me tied up because it was the perfect position. He was gone for a while. My legs were in such an awkward position, I got leg cramps and the straps hurt my ankles. I was relieved when he got back, I wanted to get it over with so I could be done and go to bed. Those were horrible times. I can't believe I ever felt sorry for him. He was always saying what a good person he was and he didn't know how else to help his problem. I needed to help him so others wouldn't be hurt. He said, society didn't help people like him and that there were a lot of men out there in the world with the same problem as his. He would apologize to me. He would cry after he was done fucking me and beg my forgiveness. He said it would make him feel better. For a reason I can't name, I knew in those moments that it was important to my survival that I never truly show how much I was hurting inside. I don't know why, but after that I kept my feelings to myself.

Years later I learned it's the little things that add up to make a person. Back then I couldn't see the little things that added up to the bigger picture of who Phillip was on the inside. I only saw what he wanted me to see. And that was a misunderstood guy with a problem that nobody wanted to help him with. I think he felt life was cheating him of what he wanted. Deep inside Phillip Garrido is a very selfish man, looking only to gratify himself as much as possible while still projecting to the world a selfless and caring man.

The first year was the worst. I hated when he would video-tape me and him having sex or me doing some other degrading thing. The camera would always have to be in the right spot and positioned just right. It was horrible. He would always assure me that the videos were just for him and nobody else would ever see them. He used them, he said, to give me a break. Years later when the sex became not as frequent, he said that he had de-stroyed the tapes and got rid of them. I believed him. Little did I know they were still on the property, only partly destroyed.

We called the first room I was taken to when Phillip kidnapped me the "studio" and later when the "runs" (long days of sex) started and he introduced me to the second building in the backyard, we called that "next door."

Funny, how I can look back now, and notice how the "secret backyard" didn't really look so "secret." It wasn't even that well hidden. I was in the middle of a neighborhood. There were neighbors all around; the only thing that was camouflaged was the gate leading to the second backyard. I can't understand why Phillip's parole officers didn't know anything about the property and the size of it. It makes me believe no one cared or was even really looking for me. Below is a diagram.

Nancy

I'm so hungry that's all I can think of. There is nothing good on television. It's so nice having a TV to watch whenever I want to; I really shouldn't complain. After the last "run," he let me stay "next door." It's a lot bigger than the studio room I was in before. There is lots of stuff to explore in here. Phillip has started to call me Snoopy. When I asked him why he said because I ask a lot of questions and he knows I've been snooping around his desk in here. He laughs and doesn't seem to mind. I wonder how he knew I had gone through his desk? It frightens me how he seems to know everything. This room has windows, too, but they have iron bars on them just like the door. He keeps the towels on them. At first when he let me stay in this room he would hand-cuff me to the pullout bed. It was really uncomfortable, but at least I got to watch the color TV. Now it's been a few months and he doesn't handcuff me anymore. I can get up and walk around. I looked out the windows but can't really see much out of them. I can see the studio, as Phillip calls it, from the outside. It looks like a barn to me. It's brown wood with many panels. Lots of wires going to and from it. I like this room better. There is more room and it doesn't feel as small as the other room.

Phillip is at the door. When he comes in, he says he has someone that wants to meet me. Behind him stands a short woman with long dark hair. Phillip introduces her as Nancy, his wife. Phillip wants us to be good friends. He tells me Nancy will bring me dinner for now. They don't stay long. Phillip comes in a little while later and tells me that Nancy is just a little jealous of me but that she will come around to liking me in time if I am good and make an effort to encourage her to like me. I can't believe he has a wife and that she helped him take me. I am young and still believed in love and that in a marriage you are faithful to each other. This is another new lesson. I figure she must be jealous because he is using me for sex instead of her. While Phillip was talking to me about Nancy, he says she doesn't really like sex and that I am helping her out, too. I really hate it and wish I didn't have to. I don't understand why I have to help her.

The first time I was introduced to Nancy, I was glad for the company. Except at first she didn't stay long. She started to bring me my meals. And Phillip would tell me that he was encouraging her to talk to me and be my friend but that she was jealous of me.

They got me a Nintendo, which is fun. I'm not as alone as I used to be. Nancy and Phillip sleep in the pullout couch. I have a pallet on the floor. Nancy came in the other day and said she had been looking for a special bear for me and she said she finally found the perfect one. She hands me a soft, squishy purple bear. I told her I loved him and I would try to think of a name for him. I think I will name him Nurple Bear. I hug him close every night. I think Nancy is starting to like me more. I'm not really sure how I feel about her. She sometimes spends time with me and tells me about her job. She works with old people at a convalescent home. She has a favorite client. He's an old Italian man named Mr. Giovetti. She likes when she gets to take care of him. She tells me that the family really appreciates the care she gives him. I hope she comes to bring me dinner soon.

Sometimes when Phillip stays up for days and days and goes on a "run," he talks about bringing Nancy in to "party with us." I do not like the sound of that at all. How could I look at her the same way if I had to have sex with her, too? That would be disgusting. I hope she feels the same way. Phillip says he's been trying to convince her. I really pray that she doesn't agree. Phillip also wants to watch his dog, Cesar, have sex with me. He says a dog's penis is not as long as his and it wouldn't hurt me as bad. I hope he is just talking and doesn't mean he will actually bring his dog in. It's one of the Dobermans that he said patrolled the backyard. He said the male, Cesar, is not very aggressive; it is the female, Hera, that was mean. He has thoughts and ideas that I have never thought of before. Why would anyone have sex with a dog? How did Phillip get such crazy ideas? I don't want to be here. I want to go home to my mom.

There is a mini-fridge in here and they have put cartons of chocolate milk and regular milk. Phillip says his mother works as a janitor at a school and she brings them home for him. There is also cereal for me to eat in the morning. Phillip loves cereal. I often hear him get up in the middle of the night having a bowl. It's very annoying, because I don't like being woken up in the middle of the night and he constantly hits the bowl with his spoon and makes a loud dinging, scraping sound. Sleep is the only escape I have. When I don't dare think, I dare to dream.

The days are so boring. I wonder what Phillip does all day. I like to make things; with the empty cartons of milk I have figured out how to make a Barbie couch and chairs. I cut the sides and then tape them into a shape I like, add cotton balls for cushion, and then glue fabric on the outside and voilà! Instant Barbie furniture. Nancy brings me things that I ask for when she can. She brings me *Disney* magazine and *Highlights* magazine, too. Nancy gave me a Birthday Barbie a few days after my twelfth birthday. An odd thing happened on my actual birthday a few days ago. Phillip comes in while I am watching TV and they say that he and Nancy have a surprise for me. I get excited thinking that they remembered my birthday and thought they had a present for me. He tells me to close my eyes while Nancy comes in and I'm thinking she is hiding my present. When Phillip says I can open my eyes, I see Nancy sitting on the end of my bed with a slight grin on her face. She is staring right at me. I interpret this to mean something, but I'm not sure why she is staring at me so intently. I look around the room expecting to see something wrapped up, but I don't see anything changed. Phillip says, "Well, can you find the surprise?" I get up to investigate the room. I finally sit back down and look at him and say I can't find anything. He says, "No, silly, it's right in front of you." I look in front of me and only see Nancy. I'm starting to feel really bad for not seeing my surprise that is supposed to be right in front of me. I shrug my shoulders and just sit and wait for them to tell me. All the while Nancy is turning her head this way and that and shaking it. Finally, Phillip points to Nancy and says, "Look at Nancy's hair." I look and see it's not long like it used to be and it is highlighted with red streaks. Nancy tells me, "Surprise. I have a new hairdo that I wanted you to see." I try to cover my disappointment with a smile and I tell her it looks great. I feel awkward and selfish for thinking that they had brought me something. I hope they don't notice how disappointed I am.

I miss my mom. My mom used to make me Barbie clothes. She had just made me some new outfits right before I went away. I wonder what she is doing right now. Does she miss me as much as I miss her? I try really hard not to think of things that make me sad. I do like to replay memories of home in my head. I don't want to forget. I'm afraid I won't remember what my mom looks like. I don't want to picture her in my head and yet at the same time I do. I miss the times when it used to be just me and her and she would scratch my back or make me macaroni and cheese. I miss her singing "You Are My Sunshine" to me and making me little things like Barbie clothes and kissing me good night.

I don't want to forget times with my aunt Tina, too. Like the time my aunt Tina picked me up from school and took me to see the floats from the Rose parade. That is the last time I saw her before we moved to Tahoe. I posed for a picture for her that day. I probably looked so goofy with my tongue out as she snapped the picture. I miss her so much right now. She was always there when I was little. She taught me how to make my first twist ponytail in my Barbies' hair. When she moved out from my grandma and grandpa's house where we lived together, she would still come and take me to her new place for a sleepover. Our favorite movie to watch together is *The Little Mermaid*. I wonder if she thinks of me. Will I ever see her again? Will anything ever be the way it's supposed to be?

Reflection

It wasn't until I wrote the last paragraph on birthdays that I realized how little I remembered my own birthdays during my years of captivity. I think I told them about my birthday and that's why Nancy gave me the birthday Barbie, but other than that I don't remember anything about that day. The birthdays I do remember were the ones marked with the ironic gift of a new tent. During those early years there was no cake, no friends, and no memories to remember.

Speaking of birthdays, this was me on my first birthday.

After the first year, things changed and we all started to spend more time together. Phillip eventually rented movies and bought fast food, he would pick up Nancy from work, and we would all sit on the pullout bed and eat a smorgasbord of fast food and watch movies. The ones I remember watching were scary like *Nightmare on Elm Street*. I also remember watching *Teenage Mutant Ninja Turtles*. I loved the old *Star Trek* series that was usually on late at night, too. Eventually I started watching *Star Trek: The Next Generation*. What I liked about *Star Trek* was that even though there was still crime in the universe, it didn't exist on earth. I liked that the earth had been cleaned up. I especially liked that future because I felt I didn't have one.

Nancy gave me a book on trees and I copied it word for word into a book I made. Nancy would always bring me something new when she came to check on me, like a new book or new crayons. This made me think she was really starting to like me. I thought she was so nice to take the time to come and see me even though she said it was hard for her. I had my own standing toilet with a built-in bucket. Phillip would empty it outside somewhere in the yard, he said. This took me a little bit to get used to. I had never used anything but a regular toilet that flushed. I thought it was gross that he was putting that kind of waste in the yard but grew used to it over time. With time, I grew used to all kinds of things. Sometimes my bucket would get so full that I would have to hold it in when I had to go. I remember one time I had to go so badly that I did it in the garbage can. Toilet paper was scarce, too. I would reuse some of the ones that just had dried pee; I know that sounds gross, but what do you use when you have to go and don't have anything? No running water, no way to go get what you need? I used what I had. I survived. There was this daddy longlegs spider up in the corner of the ceiling next to the toilet. I named her Bianca and I would talk to her (maybe I watched *Charlotte's Web* a few too many times). I was eleven or twelve at the time and had a very active imagination.

Sometimes I feel bad for not missing Nancy. But for the most part it is a relief for me to not have to endure her moods and the jealousy she harbored. She did have several opportunities to let me go, and I might never know why she chose not to.

Easter: Phillip on an Island

Nancy comes to bring me dinner. She says it's a special Easter dinner. Its 1993. I am thirteen years old. I do not feel thirteen. I still feel eleven. I don't feel like a teenager. Dinner is corned beef and cabbage. It's good. Usually they bring me fast food. So it's nice when I get a home-cooked meal. I tell her I'm so lonely to please stay and chat for a little bit and she says she will. I have asked her in the past to stay, but sometimes she says she can't because she feels guilty for taking me. She says it's hard for her to be with me. She tells me she wished and prayed the morning they took me that Phillip would get a migraine and not be able to go through with it. I think to myself, Me, too. As I finish my dinner she tells me about her day at work at the old folks' home. She says she enjoys her job but doesn't like all the girls she works with. She says they gossip a lot. She tells me that Phillip is so sweet, how he comes to visit her on her breaks and brings her flowers. Sometimes they go back to the van and smoke weed or she takes a hit of the pipe with crank in it. She says the crank helps her stay thin. She doesn't want to get fat. I think that's weird she spends so much time worrying about her weight. I don't think Phillip helps with her image when he talks about the other girls that look at him. The two of them have such a strange relationship.

She asks me things like what music I like and I tell her I like Disney songs. I also like Mariah Carey, Wilson Phillips, and Whitney Houston. I just want her to like me. I really hope she likes me. For some reason I get the feeling she doesn't like me. She says after a while that she needs to go but will be sleeping with me back here tonight. There was a movie she wanted to watch called *The Unborn;* she said she liked scary movies. So I acted like I wanted to see it. I didn't really want to watch a scary movie, but I wanted her to be happy with me. I expected to see Phillip sometime during the day, but he never came in. I tried to think of the last time I had seen him and decided it had been a few days at least. I wonder where he was. I was relieved for the release from the sex, but I knew the longer he went without it, the longer the next "run" would be. I feared his return.

That night, Nancy comes in and locks the iron door behind her. I thought it was strange because she usually slept wherever Phillip slept. I asked where he was. She said he went to live on an island with a rich friend for a while. She said he'd be gone for a month. Wow! A WHOLE MONTH WITH NO SEX! I am so excited inside. But she looks sad, so I just say, "Fine." The movie starts and it's scary and kind of disgusting with the baby walking around and killing people. Yuck! Then we hear a noise outside and we both jump. Nancy says she's scared to go see what it was but thinks she better, so she unlocks the door and goes outside. She's back in less than a minute and says everything looks okay. That the dogs were not barking, so everything must be okay. She says I can sleep with her in the big bed, and I'm grateful because I didn't want to sleep alone. By now the pullout couch has been replaced with a real mattress. I like it a lot better because it doesn't squeak like the other pullout couch did. We go to bed. In the morning she wakes up and leaves. I probably won't see her until dinnertime. The loneliness sets in again.

A few weeks later when Phillip returns, he comes "next door" where I am being kept. I actually feel happy to see him. He has been gone awhile. I missed having someone to talk to. Nancy doesn't say much and she cries a lot. It is hard to know what she wants, and I don't quite know what to say to her at times. She reminds me of a turtle; you can never quite know what a turtle is thinking. Phillip is easier to relate to; at least I know what he is thinking. Phillip makes me laugh with all his jokes and antics. He says he learned so much while he was away. He has come back with a device on his ankle, which I find strange. He tells me that he was sent back to prison for the month. He wasn't really on an island with a rich friend. He said the police had found some drugs in the house and arrested him for parole violation. He added it was Nancy's pipe that they had found. She had forgotten that she had put it in a drawer in the house. He asked if Nancy had taken good care of me and I said yes. He talked for a while longer and then took a nap on the bed, while I read quietly, wondering inside would this be the end of him hurting me? Somehow knowing it wasn't.

Christmas

The *Today* show says that today is December 25, 1993. It is day 907 of my captivity. It is Christmas Day. I am alone. I am mostly always alone. No one to talk to; no one to hug me unless Phillip comes in. He gives me hugs sometimes and makes me feel loved. But am I really? Will I always feel this alone? I try not to dwell on the things I don't have. Phillip thanks me for helping him with his problem. He said he is reading the Bible now and God is helping him, too. I hate the sex so much, but at least it's not as bad as last year. Phillip has made the "runs" a lot shorter and he hasn't been taking any drugs in between. He says he's trying to quit. The last "run" was a couple of weeks ago. Sometimes he comes in for a quick masturbation, but at least he doesn't always stick it in me. He says he saves it now for the "runs." I hate drugs, I wish he wouldn't take them. I think they turn him into another person. He seems nice the rest of the time. That's how I get through the sex, I just tell myself it will be over and he will come back and be the "nice" person I think he can be. I just have to get past feeling the pain.

He seems to have an opinion on everything, especially religion. Ever since he came back from his stay at the prison he has been reading the Bible a lot. He says the mysteries of the Bible are becoming clear to him. He doesn't seem really religious to me. The "runs" have been really scary lately, but I'm getting used to them. At least I know what to expect. He likes to follow a routine mostly. He's been acting strange lately, though. He thinks he hears voices from the TV even when it's muted. He asks me if I can hear it, too, and I say I don't hear anything, but sometimes I'm afraid to disagree with him. He bought this device called Bionic Ears and he puts it up to the wall and puts on headphones and listens to the wall for hours. On the one hand, it's great because I don't have to jack him off or anything, but it's weird, too. What does he hear? He says he hears conversations and people's voices. I don't pay much attention, it gives me the opportunity to get some rest.

Not much is going on for Christmas today. Nancy said she would bring me a plate of Christmas dinner that Phillip's mom makes. She and Phillip said they would have eaten back here with me but his mother would be alone, so they would come in later tonight. I wonder what my mom is doing today. They are probably having a nice family dinner together. I hope she is happy. I'm sure Carl is a lot happier now that I am gone. I don't think he liked me much. I got in the way a lot. I wonder if I will ever feel happy again. I pretend I'm happy a lot, just so Phillip and Nancy don't feel bad. I've learned that having a good attitude around them makes them want to do more for me. So I keep my true feelings to myself.

My plans for the day are: 1. watch the *Today* show, 2. Play a couple hours of Super Mario Bros., 3. Take a nap, and 4. Hopefully by then it will be dinnertime. My day. Very exciting. I am so lonely. I wish I had someone to talk to. Tomorrow will probably be the same.

Reflections

During these interceding months I am moved back and forth from the "studio" to "next door" many times. I'm not sure why I was shuffled from one room to the next. I think a part of it was because he liked to have some of his friends come over and smoke weed and play music all night. I remember the music coming from the studio. It would last until the wee hours of the morning sometimes. It was so loud it was hard to sleep. I got used to hearing it and it became easier. It made me feel like he was working to improve the future, and I learned not to mind. I never saw any of the people that went in there with him. I know Nancy was in there and would have to sneak away to come over and feed me when they had company. I think it was just Phillip in there, fiddling around with his sound equipment, playing by himself. I really began to think he'd be a musician one day. He had original songs that he wrote. He said he taught himself to play guitar. He said his instrument was bass but he amazed himself how well he played the guitar and keyboard. He said he didn't really need anyone to play with him, that with the equipment he had he could be a one-man band. Nancy wanted to play the drums. She had books on the subject and she said the drums were hers. I could hear her practicing on them sometimes, too.

During one of the times I was "next door," Nancy said she was looking in the paper for another kitty for me. This time they wanted to get me a kitten. I wasn't sure I wanted another kitty. It was so hard to give up the last kitten that I really didn't want to go through that again. But in the end I didn't protest very much. Nancy found an ad for a four-week-old kitten in the *Pennysaver*, and called to inquire. Turns out the kitten had a slight cold, but I decided I really wanted this one, so they went to go get her. She was the cutest thing I had ever seen. She was fluffy and white and I named her Snowy. She was a sweet little thing. Phillip didn't want her to have the run of the room, so I had to leash her to her scratching post. I would let her off of it when he wasn't around. It was hard during "runs," though, because she would cry and meow so loudly wanting to get free. Phillip didn't want cat hair sticking to the Vaseline that he used for masturbating and to lubricate me. Eventually Snowy interfered and interrupted too much with his fantasy and he got rid of her, too.

At one time I had a small tent in the room next door to the studio. They got it for me for my birthday. (I know, ironic gift, right?) I had my own sleeping bag, a shelf which I used for a desk and bookshelf. I had my own TV in there, too. When Phillip would come in for sex, I would have to leave my little sanctuary. Phillip was a lot longer than the tent, so it didn't work for him to come in and make me have sex. He would lay a blanket on the floor "next door" and make me lay there and said he would be quick if I didn't struggle. I remember laying there with unshed tears in my eyes and looking at my little tent and longing to crawl back in. They got me another cat, which I named Eclipse. I think I had her for about a month until Phillip took her away, too. I don't remember why. I do remember I wrote a journal about her. I would chronicle all the things she did during the day. It's one of the few things I eventually received back after the police removed evidence from the property. The front looks like this:

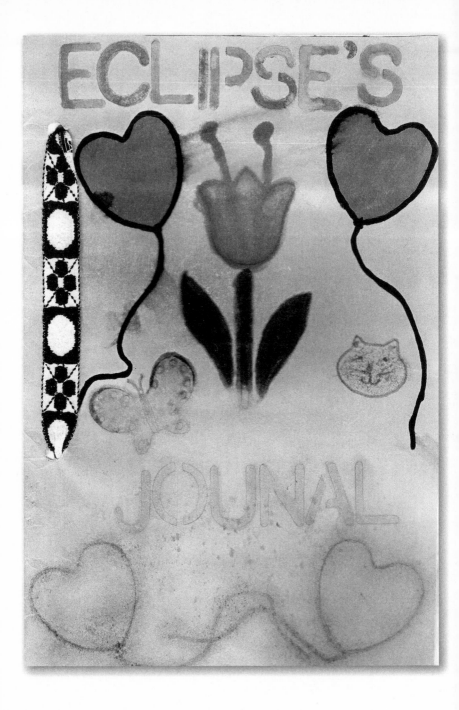

As you can see, although I've always loved writing I'm not the best speller, as this cover shows. When I got this journal back from the police and read it, I noticed I had torn the corners of the title page. It brought back the memory and how guilty I felt for writing my name in the first place. In the torn-off corner I had written: "this is written by Jaycee Dugard" on the first page of that journal. I wrote Eclipse's Journal in 1993, but already Phillip's control over my life was almost absolute. I remember, I was so proud that I had written this for my kitty and wanted to share it with someone, I showed it to Phillip and he saw that I had put my name in it. He preached to me for I think an hour about how I really didn't want to write my name, and how dangerous that could be if anyone else ever read it. I thought to myself, I never see anyone, though, but I didn't interrupt because it always ended with why he was right and I was wrong. So I tore out the corners with my name and never wrote my real name on anything again until 2009.

Monday May 3, 1993
Age - 10 weeks
height - 7 inches
length - 18 inches
Written by
for Eclipse Sweetie my new
baby Kitten
Birthday - February 23, 1993
Breed - Persian
Color of coat - gray
Color of eyes - yellow - green
Favorite food - rasins
Favorite toy - anything that rolls,
orange spring ball, purple bear

This will be the life story
of Eclipse Sweetie
Written by her best friend
for all time. my face down.
            up and rubs
            it is so very

Monday May 3, 1993
Age - 10 weeks
height - 7 inches
length - 18 inches

Today I got my new kitten at 4:00 pm. I am so happy that I have her. It took me all day before I chose the name Eclipse. I chose that name because when a total eclipse accurs it becomes dark and you can't see the moon and when Eclipse is in the dark she too disapears. Eclipse's middle name is Sweetie because when I put my face down she comes up and rubs against me, it is so very sweet. 🖤

Friday May 28, 1993
Age ~ 13 weeks

Today I'm starting this Jounal
for Eclipse. Since May 3, when I
got her, I've been very happy. I've
taught her many things she comes to
the sound of clicking of the tongue and
the sound of her bowl ringing. She
does'nt try to eat my food but I know
she wants to. Eclipse can jump very
high about four feet. I think she's
the prettiest cat in the world. I
gave her a bath but she didn't like
it. I dried her off and brushed her
coat, her coat was very shiny like
moon beams dancing on the water
at night. I gave her a friendship
bracelet, she now wears it as a
collar. I think we will be very
happy together atlest I hope so. ♡

Friday June, 4 1993
Age - 14 weeks

Thrusday the third was our one
month aniversity together. She is
growing up so fast I can't believe
it! I'm trying to teach her to stay
but it is pretty hard. She knows her
name but she won't come to it. I
know she's hungry if I pet her and
she starts to purr. I gave her a
saucer of milk she loved it, now
I give her some as a treat. She
found a way to climb to the top of
my tent she does'nt hurt it and it
is so funny. Eclipse is very special
to me because she is always with
me for me to talk to, even if
she does'nt listen I know she
cares ♡

Thursday June 10 1993
Age - 15 weeks

Eclipse is helping me fall asleep faster.
Before all I did was sit around
and watch T.V. all day, now
I watch her all day and play
with her, so by the time I go to
sleep I'm very tired and I fall right
to sleep. Last night I started to
cry and she heard me and she
came to me and sat next to
me after that I felt a little better.
If I had one wish it would be
to understand Eclipse, and she
would understand me ♡

Friday June 18, 1993
Age - 16 weeks

In my last entry I said I wish I could understand her. I suppose I can in a way, when her tail wags she is usually mad or fastrated and her pupils get real big, when she's intesested in something her tail is either straight out or down, when she is happy you can always tell, and when she's hungry her tail is straight up and her pupils are small. Eclipse absultly hates baths I have a hard time giving her one but even though she tries to get out, she has never scatched me or bit me. I'm very proud of her. I think she knows that she could of hurt me. She has scatched me a couple of time in the begining. I really think she likes me and I have no dout that I love her. ♡

Thursday June 24, 1993
Age - 17 weeks

I have nicknamed her Sweetie P, I'm
not sure why but it is pretty cute.
When I first got Eclipse I promised
her that I would never hit her I
broke my promise because I didn't
know how to make her understand me.
I know the way to make a friend is
to be a friend but I had to do it
for her safty and so I could keep
her. Now I'm pretty sure she has
learned what to do and what not
to do, so again I have made her
that promise and this time I
will not break it no matter what
she does I will always love her
with all of my heart. ♡

Saturday July, 3 1993
Age - 18 weeks

Eclipse and I are becoming
very close. I don't think
anything can break that
closeness. She knows when
I'm happy or sad. It's almost
like she has a happy meter
inside of her that lets her
know what I'm feeling and
she always makes me feel
better. She has a couple
of green balls that she
loves to play with, she
bats them around for
hours. ♡

Eclipse is purring alot more now, she purred before but only when she wanted something now she purrs because she's happy. There is a large mirror here and when she sees herself in it she thinks it's another cat and she tries to play with the image. She has a new favorite food rasins. One day I wanted to give her a treat and I found some rasins I didn't think she would like them so I put them down to look for something else, when I came back they were gone, she ate them. ♡

I think I've turned Eclipse
into a couch potato, sometimes
when there's something good
on or when she sees another
cat on the T.V. she sits in
front and literally stares at
it. She is growing so fast
I can't keep up with her
I miss her being a little kitten
but I'm glad we have built
such a strong friendship.
In the morning after she eats
she gets extremly frisky, I
have finally taught her to
stay and she does it very
well. I can't wait until
I teach her other tricks.
♡

Friday July 16, 1993
Age- 5 months

I got Eclipse for my birthday
from Phil and Nancy they
did something that no one
else would do for me,
they paid 200 dollars just
so I could have my own
Kitten. For that I could
never repay them but one
thing I know for sure
Eclipse is worth every
penny! Before I got Eclipse
I had to other cats
Tiger and Snowy, (I didn't
have them very long), Eclipse
means more to me than my
own life. When she looks
at me I see love, curiousity,
intellengee but most of all
I see her love for me.

I miss my little baby kitten
I used to hold, but now I
have a half grown kitty that
I love even more. She's
losing her baby teeth, she
has lost four so far, I'm
keeping one for sentimental
value. Almost every morning
she gets really wild and she
runs very fast around the room
If you gave the other runners
a 75 meter head start in
the one-hundred meter dash
Eclipse runs so fast she
probably would still win the
race. ♡

Tuesday July 27, 1993
Age - 5 months.

She loves to be scracted at the bottom of the tail and the nab of the neck sometimes she will start to purr. At night when it's time to go to sleep I lay down with my purple bear and Eclipse comes over paws the bear and starts to purr when she's done with the bear she comes over to me and lays down on my chest and puts her head right on my cheeks and fall asleep. She acts like she has royal blood from a princess, during the day I can't really tell if she loves me or not but not at night I can't help but know that she does love me!

Thursday August 5, 1993
Age - 6 months

Eclipse is a great fly catcher the only thing is after she catches them she eats them. One thing I know for sure is that Eclipse is a ture blue cat, she's very finiky, super playful, sleeps alot, and is very curious and smart. When there's poop in her cat box she'll scarch and scarch until I come and get in out and when there's cat food out of place she'll sniff it out and find it. I really have'nt had many cats before atleast not very smart ones except for Rusty, he was the first cat I every got so he's pretty old right now (13 years). Rusty was the smartest, bravest, caring cat I have ever know until Eclipse. They have always been there when I needed them. Eclipse reminds me of him maybe thats why I love her so much.

Rusty

Rusty was a cat that my grandma got for me when I was a baby. Rusty was around when I was growing up and living with mom, Aunt Tina, and Grandma Ninny and Grandpa Poppy. He was an orange tabby. He was an outside cat, so when me and my mom got our first apartment together I wasn't able to bring him with me, but luckily we lived about five minutes from my grandparents' house, so I was able to visit frequently. Whenever I would visit, all I would have to do is call out his name and he would come running to me no matter where he was in the neighborhood. I miss my Rusty kitty. When we moved to Tahoe, I never got to see him again.

Shortly after that last entry in Eclipse's Journal, Phillip moved me back to the studio room again. He had me pack up all the things I had in my tent in boxes and said that he was going to give

Eclipse to his aunt Celia. For what reason? I do not know. He was a very paranoid man. He said his aunt Celia absolutely adored cats and fed all the strays in her neighborhood. He said she would take very good care of Eclipse. And said if things changed in the future, maybe I could see her again one day. I never saw her again.

Looking back on that, I don't really think they spent two hundred dollars on a cat. I must have really needed to believe something good about them. I learned that by being "good" and not complaining a lot I received more freedoms along the way. It didn't usually matter what I needed. It was all about Phillip, his needs, and what he wanted. He got rid of Eclipse while he was on a "run." The "run" lasted for days, and when I was sent back "next door" Eclipse was gone. I learned never to ask questions because the answers never made me feel any better. It seemed every argument ended up with me wrong and him right. He had all the power.

I was moved back into the studio for a couple of weeks, not sure when. And then it was back "next door." I have no idea what his reasoning was for moving me back and forth. I didn't ask. I just did what I was told. I don't know what happened to Eclipse. It would be four years before I got another cat.

Learning I Was Pregnant

Easter Sunday, 1994. I have been moved back to the studio. Phillip said that he thought he had heard someone talking about police in the neighborhood and thought I would be better protected in the semi-soundproof studio. He said I had to be extra quiet when I walked around. He removed the wall that used to separate the mixing room from the music room. Now it is one big room. I have a new pallet on the floor in the back corner. There is a partition to give me a feeling of privacy. It's Easter and we have been spending the whole day together. Nancy, Phillip, and I. Phillip and Nancy have a bed in middle of the room. It is a mattress with no box spring. We have been watching *The Ten Commandments* with Charlton Heston and eating a ham dinner that Phillip's mother Pat made. They both tell me to close my eyes. When I open, I see an Easter basket. The basket is filled with candy and it also has two little Easter bunnies, a boy and a girl. I tell them thank you and that I love it. Phillip says there is something that he needs to talk to me about. He says he and Nancy have been watching me lately and noticed that I'd been putting on weight and waddling instead of walking. I said I know. I told them I did feel bigger and that I didn't realize I was walking funny. I told them my stomach was hurting a lot, too. They said, "We think you may be pregnant." I am stunned and scared. What was going to happen to me? What was going to happen to the baby? I knew babies were delivered in a hospital. After all, that was where my mom had delivered my little sister. I wonder how I could possibly have a baby in this place. I will probably have to give her up for adoption, how can I possibly raise a baby in this environment? I wonder if Phillip is happy about this baby. I don't feel like I can ask him in front of Nancy, though, so I think I will wait to ask him later. When Nancy gets upset about something, I don't see her or she doesn't talk to me for days.

A few days later, on the inside I am still haunted by the thought of having to give up the baby. I need to talk to Phillip about it soon. Phillip brings China, a beautiful blond cocker spaniel, to visit me. China belongs to his mother, Pat. He told me how he found her. He said he was at a gas station a few years back with his door open while he filled the car up with gas. All of a sudden this dog jumped in. He took her home. When his mother is away from the house at work (I learned she works at a school as the head janitor), Phillip brings China to see me. He knows I really love animals. China always makes me feel so much better. She lays her head on my ever-expanding, painful tummy. All my worries just seem to melt away. Laying there with

China next to me and feeling the baby move and kick my ribs, I come to realize that I can never give up my baby. Giving her away was not even an option. I would figure a way out before I ever gave her away. I don't know how I would do that, but I know I wouldn't stop until I did.

The connection I feel for this baby inside of me every time I feel it move is an incredible feeling. I talk to my belly and tell it stories. Every time I feel the baby kick, I feel less and less alone in this world. My body is growing every day, accommodating the baby inside of me. My ribs are being pushed out and it's very painful. I can feel my body changing. I'm not sure how far along I am, but I'm thinking I've been pregnant for a while and just didn't show right away. That's what Phillip says. He seems very happy that I'm having a baby and never brought up anything about giving it away.

Reflection

I've been thinking back about what I've been writing and I'm not so sure things went exactly the way Phillip said they went. For example, it's a load of malarkey that some random dog just happened to jump into his car at the gas station. It doesn't ring true now that I think about it. I wonder how he actually got China. At the time I had no ability to doubt him. I remember thinking, Dogs don't just jump in strangers' cars. He would always talk about how much animals loved him. He had an Irish setter named Baby. He said that she had puppies and those puppies would come running when he would make this special call. Nancy would always say how much animals really liked him, too. I never really saw it as something special, though. Animals like their owners. Even when an animal is mistreated or abused, some animals crave love and affection so much they would do anything for that attention.

China

Driving to a Trailer

I have been moved back "next door." Phillip has painted this room yellow and has put up a wall to make it into two rooms. He has given me the one with no windows.

One evening before the baby was born, Phillip came next door while I was watching TV. He said that something was going on. We need to leave the house. I haven't left this place since the day he took me nearly two years ago. I asked what was going on, but he ignored me and said that he would make sure the baby and I were safe and that I needed to listen to him. He said that someone told him there was going to be a raid on the house and it wasn't safe here right now. He said he was going to put a blanket over me and lead me to the van. I was tired and didn't want to go. What choice did I have? He controlled everything. He said Nancy was waiting in the van for us and had everything ready. I asked if I can take anything with me, and he said no and if everything goes right he will be bringing me home soon. I get up and he puts the blanket over me. I am really getting scared. What if something happens to him? What would I do? I feel like I can't catch my breath. I must breathe in and out slowly and tell myself everything will be fine. He leads me out to the van, and I climb in the back and before I can ask where he wants me to sit, he says for me to crawl under the backseat and he was going to put some boxes in front of the seat. Oh my God, that's ridiculous, I think to myself! Can't I just sit over in the corner? He says that would be dangerous. Dangerous to whom? But I don't argue; I just crawl under the seat. It's kind of hard because my belly is dragging on the floor making it very difficult. I'm afraid I might hurt the baby. I wiggle around and try to find a comfortable position. I finally settle on half on my side and forward a little 'cause the seat is kind of low. Not much wiggle room. I am so uncomfortable! I want to be in my own bed! I hear the van start and back out of the driveway. I wonder where we are heading. Phillip thinks people can hear him when he talks, so he told me earlier that whenever he addressed me it would sound like he was talking to Nancy. He doesn't want anyone to think there was another person in the van.

The driving seems endless. How long have we been driving? What time is it? When we left it was just getting dark, but now it's completely dark especially under the seat. I must have fallen asleep, for when I wake the van has stopped. He helps me to get out. He has to pull me out a bit because I am so stiff from being in the same position for so long. What a relief it is to be out from under the seat. It's still dark out. We are standing in front of a house trailer. I keep my head down as we go in. The steps are really steep. There is a couch in the living room he says I can sit there. I sit and he and Nancy check out the rest of the place. He comes back and asks if I need anything. I ask where we are. And he says this trailer used to belong to a friend named Virginia. She died and left it to him. I say I really need to use the bathroom. My bladder can't hold much since I've been pregnant. I follow him to an actual bathroom! What joy! I haven't used an actually flushing toilet in so long! And a sink with running water to wash my hands! I come out and he says I should go back to the couch. I want to explore! Explore an actual house—it's been so long! I can see a kitchen and there are bedrooms in the back. But I go sit on the couch. I ask for some water and Nancy gets it for me. Phillip says that we are going to stay the night here because the house isn't safe. I wonder what's going on in the house. Are there people in the back going through my stuff? I wonder what's going on. Phillip locks the front door and says I can sleep on the couch and he and Nancy will be in the back bedroom. It takes a while to fall asleep with all the questions in my head, but I must eventually because when I wake it is morning and Phillip and Nancy are talking in the kitchen. They must have been waiting for me to get up. When I do, they say they are going to leave me here for a few hours so that they can check out the house and get some food for me. He says I can get up to go to the bathroom, but it would be much better for me to just stay on the couch and sleep. He told me that everything would be okay and for me not to be scared because he would come back. I was so scared he wouldn't return for me and just leave me here forever by myself. What would I do all by myself and pregnant? I start to cry. I tell him I don't want to stay alone, that I am scared something would happen. He continued to say he had to go make sure the house was okay and he and Nancy would be back with something good to eat. So he and Nancy left and I heard the click of the lock. I tried to fall asleep but sleep would not come. I finally got up to go to the bathroom. I thought to myself, Since I'm up I might as well check out the rest of the place. I know he told me not to, but what harm could a little peek make? I tiptoe down the hall and think to myself, What if he finds out? He knows so many things. What if he knows I looked around? Curiosity has gotten the better of me. The first room all the way down the hall is a pretty good size, but all that it contains is a mattress on the floor. There's another room across from the bathroom. It looks like a screened-in porch. It would be so nice to have this as a room for me and the baby one day. Phillip says he is going to try to find a way to get this into the backyard so we can use it. We would have a bathroom and a full kitchen! Oh my God, it would be so wonderful. I hope he can find a way to do it. I walk back into the living room. All the furniture in here looks so old and dusty. The kitchen is pretty nice, though. I open the refrigerator and dream about actually being able to use this every day. Always to have food available, what a joy that would be! I finally settle back on the couch and fall asleep. When I wake it is to the sound of the door opening. I get scared for a minute. What if it's not them? But it is and I am so happy to see them. They have brought chili beans. Nancy heats them up on the stove and fixes me a bowl with a flour tortilla to go with it. Phillip says that it is now safe to go back home but not until it gets dark outside. They go in the back to take a nap and I stay on the couch and wait. I'm in my mind, thinking about what my life used to be like. Reliving memories is one of the ways I keep my past alive inside. I don't want to forget my family back home. I fear that one day I won't remember what my mom looks like. Already her image is fading from my mind. Soon night comes and Phil is ready to go but seems on edge again. He says he thinks it best if we drive around some more before we go home. I just want to go home. What's going on that he thinks we can't? Again he doesn't answer. I get back in the van and under the seat. After the first time I know what to expect down here, but that doesn't make it any easier. After a while of driving I start to feel really sick. I call out to them and tell them I feel like I'm going to throw up. Phillip pulls over, and Nancy comes to the back with a plastic bag. They tell me to hold on awhile longer. I try but the movement of the car brings my lunch of beans right up. The bag is too small to contain all the beans. I'm at a very bad angle to be throwing up and I don't have much room to maneuver. Throwing up does make me feel better, but now I have to lay in this awful disgusting mess. Finally Phillip announces that we are home. Nancy comes to the back and takes the bag and cleans up the rest of the puke from the carpet. Then I come out with a sheepish grin on my face and say, "I'm really sorry." I am thinking, Hey, it's not my fault. I don't see why we were driving in the first place. But of course I say nothing of the sort, I wouldn't talk back to him like that. I am glad we are home. I get cleaned up and change my clothes and go to bed in my own bed. Phillip says that whatever was going on has passed and there's nothing to worry about for now.

Reflection

I still don't know what to make of that day. I was just glad when it was over. I've always thought I am a go-with-the-flow kind of person. My mom says that my nickname was "the Bull" when I was little, but I don't remember that. She says I was real stubborn when it came to something I really wanted; that I would dig my heels in and be very persistent about whatever it was. I never thought of myself as stubborn, but looking back I can see some instances where that would fit me. In the beginning I asked a lot of questions about everything. I think I was always an inquisitive person. I learned when to back off with the questioning early on with Phillip. Sometimes not asking questions made things easier. Phillip's verbal abuse was very effective. Although I would have liked some direct answers to my questions, I learned to not question too much because the answer I got would be lengthy and in the end make me forget the question in the first place. The fact is, I do have many questions such as: Whose trailer were we using that night? What did he think he was hearing? What really happened to the person that lived there? I might never know the answers to these questions.

Waiting for Baby

I'm watching many baby shows to prepare myself to take care of a baby. Phillip started watching a lot of child care shows, too. He especially likes a gentleman on TLC; I can't remember his name, though. He has rented birthing videos from the library and watched them with me. It looks pretty scary, but he said he could do it and nothing would go wrong.

Every day seems to melt into the next. I don't know what is going to happen. All the preparation seems to melt away and I have no recollection of the day-to-day activities I did to prepare for an infant's arrival. Phillip moved me next door to what he calls "next door." I have a bed and dresser and my own TV. This afternoon as I was watching *Doctor Quinn: Medicine Woman*—it's one of my favorite shows to watch—I have been having sharp pains all day, but I didn't really think anything of it this morning; I have been in pain before. But this pain seemed different and started to get so severe by afternoon I couldn't even move. Is this what it feels like to have a baby? I wish I wasn't alone. I am so scared! No one has come to check on me all day and the door was still locked, so I have to wait until someone comes.

Nancy finally comes in around five p.m. She sees me hunched over in pain. She goes to get Phillip and he asks me all kinds of questions like, how long do the contractions last and that sort of thing while Nancy goes to get all the stuff they need, like towels and hot water. Phillip reminds me about the birthing videos and reassures me that he knows what to do. Nancy is a nurse's aide. I don't have anyone else.

The contractions last into the night. I twist and turn and try to find a comfortable position, but nothing helps. It is late by the time my water finally breaks. At first I thought I had peed myself. I tell Phillip and he thinks it won't be long now. When my water broke I felt an instant of relief from the constant pressure I had been feeling for months as the baby grew inside of me. The pressure returned after that when it was time for me to push. I have never been in so much pain in my life. Phillip tells me I need to push now. It seems like it is taking forever and the baby is still not coming. He feels inside and discovers the cord is around the baby's neck and is preventing the baby from coming out. He uses his finger to pull the cord away slightly and the next push is successful! Nancy takes her and gets her cleaned up. I still had the placenta to push out. That seems to take forever, too. After that they gave her to me to hold for the first time and cleaned up all the mess and changed my sheets. I am exhausted and all I want to do is go to sleep. I nurse her for the first time, which feels very strange to me and then we both went to sleep. My baby girl came into the world at 4:35 a.m., August 18, 1994. I am fourteen years old and very, very scared.

Reflection

Recounting that day, I can't believe that was me that went through this. I can't imagine ever going through something like this again by myself. Obviously, I didn't have a choice with the second pregnancy either. How did I not just go insane with worry? How do you get through things you don't want to do? You just do. I did it because that was the only thing I could do. I would do it all again. The most precious thing in the world came out of it . . . my daughters.

I'm not sure why Phillip chose the name he did for my first daughter, which later in his delusional thinking began to symbolize the powerful spirit forces that controlled his mind. I have my own reason for not protesting the name she was given. To me her name symbolizes everything good in the universe. It encompasses my old beliefs and helped me hold on to those beliefs even when I was hit the hardest with his "angel theory." I don't think of myself as a religious person. Even with all the many hours Phillip insisted we sit and listen to his interpretation of the Bible, I still don't really know if I believe in the Bible at all. When I was little, before I was taken away by Phillip, one of my favorite things to collect were these figures called "Precious Moments." They came in all kinds of shapes and sizes, and each one had a unique quote on a locket necklace. I received a Guardian Angel Precious Moment for my ninth birthday. I kept it in its stand atop my dresser.

Taking Care of a Baby

My beautiful baby girl. This photo was taken "next door."

It is two a.m. in the morning. A will not go to sleep. She is only quiet when I stand up and bounce her on my shoulder. Will she ever sleep through the night? My breasts hurt so much from her nursing. I have told Phillip. He said he would talk to a pharmacist. Hopefully he can find something for me to use to make them feel better. I have a new rocking chair that Phillip found at the Salvation Army. It is all one smooth line, with this peach fabric covering it. It's so ugly! But I am grateful to have it. A loves to be rocked. I rock her for hours and hours and sing "You Are My Sunshine" just like my mom used to sing to me. Nancy got me a tape cassette player and some of my favorite Disney music. Phillip also gave me some of his songs on tape that he made. I think I will put them on for A and see if that will get her to sleep. I like to keep her on a schedule as much as I can. She wakes up about nine a.m. for feeding and then we both go back to sleep until about noon for another feeding, then we will play for a little bit. Games like peekaboo and this little piggy. She is about three months now and growing every day. She has the biggest eyes I've ever seen. I wonder if she will grow into them. I like to give her a bath a little before bedtime to help her sleep. Phillip put a microwave in the other room. I use it to heat up some water in an old wipes container. There is no sink in here, but Phillip buys those big water containers, so I usually have plenty of water to bathe the baby and brush my teeth at night. I have a baby bath to put her in and clean towels and washcloths. Nancy and Phillip get me whatever I need for the baby. I have toys and clothes and plenty of diapers and wipes. Sometimes the baby gets a diaper rash and I use Desitin to clear it up. She seems very healthy, though, and inquisitive.

Life's a lot nicer than it used to be since the baby came. Phillip hasn't made me have sex with him since the baby came and no "runs" either. When I was pregnant he didn't make me have sex, but one time I had to take off my shirt and masturbate him.

Phillip and Nancy come in to visit a lot more, too. Sometimes they take A in the studio with them. That is where Phillip and Nancy are sleeping. I think Nancy likes to pretend that A is her baby. I like the break from the baby because we are together 24/7, but I am also a little jealous. I want some attention, too.

I am so lonely. Sometimes I dream about my friends that I used to have. Especially my very first friend, Jessie. We met in 1984 when I was four and she was three. My mom and I had just moved into an apartment complex together. It was just me and her. Before then I had lived with her at my grandma's house. I was so happy to be living with her in our own place. Just the two of us. One day I was playing outside in the courtyard and another little girl came outside to play, too. She had long dark brown hair and was very skinny. She came over to where I was inspecting the juniper bush for ladybugs (my favorite pastime). She came over and started to look, too. I pulled a ladybug off the bush and showed it to her and then put it on her hand. It fell to the ground and when she went to pick it up she accidentally squished it. I started to cry and she started to cry, too. As our moms started to come over to see what was wrong, she very gently took another ladybug from the bush and offered it to me. I looked at it for a minute and then smiled and accepted her gift. After that we were inseparable and our moms became friends, too. I miss her now more than ever.

When we got older and I was sent to live with my aunt and uncle for the year, Jessie would always send me special things. Like one time she sent me this bear that had a secret spot in the back where you could hide special things. I loved that bear and I loved Jessie, too, for not forgetting me. I wonder what her life is like now. I always thought we were the same but different. She was thin and I was pudgy. She was outgoing and not shy, and I was shy and quiet. We both lived with our moms. No dads in our lives. I wonder if we would still be friends if I was home. I wish I could go home. I do not ask to go home anymore. Too painful to even think about. I just hope one day things will get better. I can't imagine staying here until I'm old and gray, but yet I don't know what the future holds for me. All I have is Phillip and he always seems to know what to do. Where would I go with a baby? Who would want me?

Sarge

It is 1996. A is a toddler now. Phillip fixed up the room with the bars on it for us to live in pretty much permanently. I'm still not allowed to leave the room, but Phillip has been slowly working on fencing in the backyard. He says it's so A and I could get some sun. I am looking forward to that.

Nancy brought a cockatiel home from work today. It was midafternoon and I thought she was coming in with dinner. I was surprised when she had a birdcage in her hand instead of dinner. She said a girl from work gave it to her because her son and daughter were not taking care of him. I could see she was right from the big flop of super glue the gray-and-yellow bird had on the top of his beak and the bare spots on his chest where he had plucked out his feathers. This told me that he was not a happy fellow. Nancy said that it was her bird but thought that I might like to keep it in here for a while. I was grateful, thinking maybe

I could teach it to talk and then I'd have someone else to talk to. Nancy said the bird was really mean and that I should not try to touch it. I thought to myself that all he needs is time to trust me and maybe he will grow to like me. I had started forming a plan almost immediately in my head, but I didn't voice my thoughts out loud. I asked if he had a name, and Nancy said not yet. I told her maybe we could watch him and see if a name fit his behavior. As the days passed I talked to my new roommate every day. And I put my hands by the cage, too. The frightened cockatiel would become very agitated each time he saw my hand was near and always backed as far away as he could. When I put new food in his cage, he would always try to bite me. I let him most of the time because it didn't hurt too much and I wanted him to know I wasn't afraid of him. On weekends, when Nancy was home, she would come and get him when it was warm outside and say that he needed some fresh air and she was going to hang him up in the sunshine. I envied his time in the sun. Sometimes when she came in with dinner I would remind her to bring him in. Usually after he was back inside, my efforts to befriend the silly guy would continue. After a few weeks of constantly trying to get him used to my hand, I got brave one day and I put my hand in the cage. When he tried to bite me, I gently pushed his beak away and said no, no. I did this every day and slowly but surely after about a week I was able to have my hand in the cage with no protesting. About this time I was starting to call him Sergeant, or Sarge, for short. He would pace back and forth in his cage and it reminded me for some reason of an army sergeant. So that's what I called him. Sarge was a great singer; he especially liked music and would sing aloud whenever he heard a tune. I first noticed it as I was singing A to sleep and couldn't really hear myself for the noise of one singsong bird. He would whistle and carry on to the radio, too. As the days went by, his feathers grew back and the glue on his nose peeled off. Sergeant became much happier and would even sit on my finger. I would take him out of his cage and he would march back and forth on the floor and make me and the baby laugh and laugh. I didn't really want to show Nancy what I had taught Sarge to do. I thought she might take him away or be jealous. Whenever Phillip would come and I brought out Sarge, he would be amazed at the transformation from angry, mean bird to proud marching, singing bird. He also thought that I shouldn't make too big of a deal about it to Nancy. He thought she might get upset that I had not listened when she said I couldn't touch the bird. I said to him that she just said I shouldn't touch him because he bites, not that I couldn't. I didn't want to cause trouble and I really wanted Nancy to like me. I had come to love that proud little gray-and-yellow marching bird and hoped I could keep him as my own, but was too shy to ask Nancy and wished she wouldn't take him away.

Summer came and went and fall slipped in. Nancy wasn't taking Sergeant out as much because it was getting colder. But one day she came in and said she thought it was warmer than usual and would take him out for an hour or two and bring him back. I was watching TV and not really paying attention. Later that day Nancy brought dinner in and left. I didn't get a chance to remind her of the bird. After I ate I returned to watching TV and didn't think about Sergeant until I was getting ready for bed. I noticed no cage in the corner. I wondered if Nancy forgot. I had no way of contacting her next door; they always locked the iron door so there was no way I could go get him. I kept getting up and looking out the window as I pulled the towel aside. Where were they? I didn't see any lights on in the studio. Did Phillip say he was going on a "run" tonight with Nancy? I couldn't remember if he had told me anything. I watched TV to keep my mind from thinking the worst. I hoped Sergeant was alright. I feared he'd freeze if left out for much longer. Finally, Nancy came in with him and he looked okay. Nancy felt bad that she forgot to bring him in earlier. She and Phillip went to get some speed from a friend. Sarge looked to be okay and was whistling up a storm. She said she could hear him squawking all the way to the front yard. That's how she remembered that she had forgotten to bring him inside. After she left, I told Sarge how sorry I was that he was left out in the dark and gave him a sprig of millet for a peace offering. He didn't touch it and settled on his perch for sleep, so I covered his cage with a towel. A and I went to sleep, too.

The next morning I knew something was wrong the minute I woke up. Every other morning I woke up to sounds of little feet on newspaper. Typing on the computer keys reminds me of his little feet on the bottom of his cage. But this morning I heard nothing but silence. I sat on the side of the bed for a while, not wanting to know why I heard no noise from Sergeant. I finally worked up the courage to peek in the cage. I saw my beloved marching bird dead on the bottom of his cage. I don't know why, but I had to touch him one last time so I put my hand in and touched him. He was cold. I cried a lot that day. The hardest part was waiting for Phillip and Nancy to come in so I could tell them Sarge had died. When Phillip finally came in, I started crying and told him Sarge got cold and died. He at first didn't think it was due to the cold but didn't know what else it could have been either. I didn't see Nancy that day. Later I learned she couldn't face me because she thought I blamed her. I do.

Second Baby

I am pregnant again. I was so afraid it would happen again. He's only been on a few "runs" these last few years. He hasn't been taking as many drugs. And he seems to have a steady job working at a nursery for a guy he calls Marvin. Marvin lets him take home lots of wood and stone steps, too. Phillip still says that he is going to put up a tall fence so I can go outside and enjoy the sunshine. I think A enjoys going outside, too. Nancy sometimes takes her outside to play, but I can't go because they are afraid someone will see me. I don't want to get them in trouble. Where would I go if they were gone? Would Nancy let me go if Phillip wasn't around? I don't think she would because she didn't let me go when Phillip was sent back to prison that one month. She had the opportunity then, and I didn't even know it. It sure would be nice to go outside once in a while. Phillip has built a room outside of the room I'm in. Even though it is outside, I still can't go anywhere else without Phillip or Nancy. This new room is enclosed on three sides, and he has put my toilet in there along with the mini-fridge, and he has hooked up a sink. I can get water. Sometimes I go sit on the pot while A is playing inside just to get a little break from her. I know this is wrong and I shouldn't mind being with her all day, but it is so overwhelming at times. When she realizes I am gone, she starts to bang on the door and I tell her I will come in when I'm finished with the bathroom, but she throws a fit and screams and acts like she can't bear to be away from me. She's usually a good girl, but when she has a tantrum about something I just don't know what to do. Nancy said I should set up a chair in the corner and make her sit there. I did try that, but she just gets up and does what she wants. She's very headstrong. Our days are usually spent playing together. She has a myriad of toys that Nancy and Phillip have brought her. She likes watching *Sesame Street* and *Barney* in the mornings, and I like to teach her ABCs. She's three now and I'm still breast-feeding her, which is hard, because she is bigger now and has teeth. I constantly have to tell her to not bite me. Phillip says I am doing the best thing that I could possibly do for her by breast-feeding.

I don't know how I know I'm pregnant again, but I know I am. My body has this full feeling. The last time he made me have sex with him, he didn't pull out in time and the semen went in. He said this time would be the last time ever. I don't know if I can believe him because he has said that many times before. He says he's been working on his problem and that I won't have to suffer anymore. I don't know what has made him say he is going to stop. I know it is something I have always wanted him to do. I hate it. Each and every time. There is no enjoyment for me, even though he says one day I will enjoy it. I wonder how he will feel about another baby. I know he loves A and swears to God that he would never harm her in any way. He said he was holding her in his arms in the studio one day and he prayed to God and cried out, "God, please don't ever let me hurt this little girl." He said God cured him of his sexual problem and that's why he says he will never touch me again. I want to believe him, but it's hard to believe that he will never touch me again. Sometimes I dream about running away, but I have nowhere to go. And now I will have another baby.

I can hear the van. The van that Phillip drives has a very loud motor and although I have never seen it, I can hear when he leaves and comes home again. It reminds me of the commercial on TV about the Dodge vans having "Hemi" engines. Hemi engines are very loud. I can hear the van when it comes or goes. At times I feel anxious when I hear the van leave. Mixed feelings make my pulse accelerate. I like it when he is gone, but I worry about being alone. I know he will always return. I don't know how I feel about that either. I do not want to be alone, but when he is gone, there is no sex to worry about. I have not left this place since the "trailer home" drive.

When he comes in with fish and chips from Jack in the Box, I smile and say thank you. He says he has a surprise and says I am going to go to the studio so that he and Nancy can put it together. I tell him that I have been feeling sick and that I think I am pregnant again, and he says he knows and that he will take care of everything. He says he's really happy and that he knows it's going to be another girl because God knows that's what he needs. I am seventeen years old and about to have my second baby.

I go to the studio and play with the baby for a while, and when they come back hours later, I follow them back into my room and to my surprise see a big red bunk bed. It is humongous. The bottom bunk is a full size and the top is a twin. The bottom sticks out about two feet from the top bunk, so there is room for me to sit without bumping my head. There's a ladder that leads up to the top bunk, and A wants to climb it. Phillip helps her up and she is excited to be up so high. They ask if I like the color and I say yes, I do, even though I don't really like red. I would have preferred blue or black or even silver. But they both thought that I'd really like the red color. The room looks even smaller now. I think about how there is not much room for A to play anymore; but, oh well, it is a nice bed. I'm also a little bummed because now I can't rearrange the room too much anymore; that was one of my most favorite things to do to make the room look different from time to time 'cause everything is so much the same.

Phillip has been working outside on the fence every day and it is finally done. I am so excited to go outside. I will have so much more freedom now. Nancy is here, too, and says I should close my eyes so it will be a surprise. I close my eyes and as Phillip takes A and I take Nancy's hand and we walk out together into the sunshine, I can feel it, the sun, warm on my face. There is an old picnic table and bench out here. And Phillip and Nancy say that we can have barbecues out here and be a real family. I am really looking forward to having a family and doing things again. I have been cooped up for so long. There's also an old dresser out here, too, and on it is a cute little guinea pig in a cage. He's so cute. Phillip says it's for me. He said his neighbor, J., didn't want him anymore. He said she has so many animals, she asked Phillip if he wanted a guinea pig. I pick him up and he squeals a little. I show him to A and she starts to laugh and rub her nose in his soft fur. I have been watching this new TV show lately called *7th Heaven*. The family in it has a dog named Happy. I think I will name the guinea pig Happy.

Nancy doesn't seem to like the name I've chosen for the guinea pig. She keeps calling it Guinevere, even though it's a boy. I think it's weird. But she can call it whatever she wants, I guess. Nancy seems strange to me sometimes. But I still really want her to like me. Phillip says he has many talks with her and encourages her to be my friend more. I wonder if that will ever happen. Sometimes she tells me how much she hates the summertime. She says Phillip and she will drive to school playgrounds and parks and videotape little girls. Sometimes she has to entertain little girls and get them to do the splits and sit with their legs apart so he can videotape it secretly. She says the camera is hidden, and one time he cut a piece out of her purse and put the camera in there. So weird and disgusting, I think. He said he was working on his sex problem. It doesn't seem to me that he is. I know he still smokes crank and weed with Nancy and he uses the videos to masturbate with. I still don't understand his problem. All I know is that he has one. At least there are no more "runs" for me for now. I hope he leaves those other kids he videotapes alone.

The Starting of Printing for Less

Phillip has rented a computer from the rental store. Phillip has also bought a Canon printer. He has plans to start his own business. He says many people are in need of business cards, and he says he wants to start a business and make them for a lot less than other companies. His first job comes from his old boss, Marvin, from the nursery. Phillip quit that job around the time that he finished the fence. Nancy once told me that before that job, Phillip worked at the convalescence home she worked at as a janitor. She said everyone loved him there, but that the manager had to fire him for coming in late too many times. It was because he was always doing drugs. Nancy said that's the reason they fired her, too. One too many times coming in late. She found another job working at a program called CAP (Client Assistance Program). She loves her new job she says. Working with the "clients," as she was told to refer to the disabled people, is really fun, she says. She says one of the clients named Bernard is really loud and yells everything but is a very sweet person. She doesn't like the other workers there too much, except one named B who doesn't gossip too much. Phillip eventually wants her to stop working when the new baby comes. He wants to have the printing business up and running by then.

I like the computer. It's so new and can do so many things. He had an older computer, but it was black and white and very old. This one is amazing. Phillip lets me come travel from "next door" to the studio at certain times of the days now, like when Nancy is at work. I bring the baby over, too. I play with A on the computer. Phillip has bought a few learning games for the computer. One is a *Sesame Street* letter and counting game. A is learning so much. When she has a nap, I learn a lot about the computer, too. It is color and has an operating system called Windows. Phillip has bought a program to make the business cards on called Corel Print House. I like to make things for the baby with it. I am putting together a scrapbook, and I also like to write stories with the program called Word. I think I can make designs look better than Phillip can. He has showed me some of the business cards he has made, and I think I can make them better. I think I can improve the cutting, too. His are not cut right because he wants to get it done in a hurry and tries to cut ten sheets at once. I think he should cut one at a time. He says that would take too long. I tell him, no, it won't and ask if I can try one sheet and see. He lets me try and I am able to make a pretty good cut. I have the idea if I put tiny lines for me to see to cut on it would make it much easier. So I try that on the computer and print a new sheet and they are much easier to cut. They look good, too. The next day he brings home my first job. It is a wedding announcement for someone. I work up a design and he takes it to the customer and gets it approved. When he brings it back to me, I print them on the cards the woman has selected to use. The job turns out great and I am very proud of myself. Phillip says that he thinks I should do the workups and he will get the jobs and help with the printing. I continue to learn and get better using the computer, and Phillip brings in more and more jobs. It's so nice to not be bored all the time like before.

Birth of Second Baby

On November 12, 1997, I awake at eleven p.m. in terrible pain. The pain has come out of nowhere. I don't remember feeling bad the previous day. A is asleep beside me and I know I must wake her up and bring her with me next door to the studio, where Phillip and Nancy are sleeping. At least I hope they are sleeping. I know the night before they were on a "run," but I hope they are done for now because I think the baby is coming.

I shake A up and tell her that the baby is coming and we need to go to Daddy. I hope that Phillip doesn't get mad that I am coming to wake him up, but as the pain gets more unbearable I have no choice. I start the walk over with A's hand in mine. When we walk the few feet over to the next building, I must let go of A's hand for a second and use both hands to yank the heavy studio door open. Sometimes during the day when I am alone

I stand and stare at this door that once was my prison. I am in another kind of prison now. Free to roam the backyard but still prisoner nonetheless. I feel I am bound to these people—my captors—by invisible bonds instead of constant handcuffs. No one seems to care that I am there.

As I finally get the door open and once again gather A's hand, I help her up the steps and into the warm room beyond. It is dark and I fear falling, so I flick on the light. Phillip has once again erected the wall that used to be my first prison and is now the room they use to sleep in. He has made the top shelf that once held one of his keyboards into a bed and the bottom part is another bed. He has sold or pawned most of his music equipment away for drug money and diapers. He is sleeping in the top bunk as I shake him awake with a smile on my face and hope in my heart that I will not get in trouble, but also not really caring at the moment. He comes awake with a start; he must have been sleeping heavy. He asks what the matter is and I tell him I think the baby is coming. He wakes Nancy and they fly into action. Nancy going to the house to get towels and hot water, and he's getting the first aid kit and whatever else he needed for the delivery. He tells me not to worry; he knew what to do. The contractions were coming closer and closer now and I really just wanted to lie down. Nancy came back and is making me a place for me to lie. I lie down and feel much better. The lights are so bright after just waking up, but I know Phillip needs to be able to see. He feeds me ice chips and puts cool compresses on my head. I take codeine for the pain. I didn't really want to take anything that would hurt the baby, but Phillip assured me that there were no lasting effects to the baby from codeine. I had taken it with A and she was fine. Nancy turned the TV on for her and entertained her so she wouldn't worry about me. I could hear her in the other room asking all sorts of questions. All I could think of was me, though, and how much it hurt.

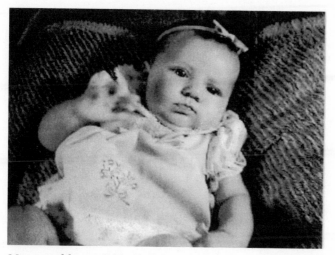

My second beautiful baby girl

It wasn't long before I was pushing the baby out. With A it felt like I was in labor forever. This one seemed to be going by so fast. In a matter of hours I gave birth to my second daughter at 2:15 a.m. November 13, 1997. Phillip later named her S. Nancy and Phillip wanted me to pick a name out of the Bible for her middle name. Nancy suggests Ruth or G, and I like G better. Phillip is reading the Bible a lot more now. I'm not sure what he is looking for. It gives him a focus and I am thankful for that. Phillip says that he has torn up the Bible two times now. One time he threw the pages in his bucket, which he uses to go number two in outside. He said he was fed up with God at one point and didn't think he would ever pick up the Bible again. Well, something must have changed because he has a new Bible now called NIV. I see him reading and talking to Nancy about it every time I see them. He is mentioning Bible studies for me and Nancy. Phillip says that with God's help he is coming to understand the voices that he hears, and God has cured him of his sexual problem. I will believe that when I see it.

Reflection

The night before I am to testify in front of a grand jury I had this dream . . .

I was in this interview room with Phillip and Nancy. Phillip was behind this big desk to my right and Nancy was sitting in a smaller desk straight in from of me. I was sitting in a swivel chair in the center of the room. Phillip was asking me all these question that I can't remember and I was smirking at him and telling him I wasn't going to answer any of his questions because I didn't have to. He then said it looked like I needed a hug and when he started to get up, I yelled for the officer who was supposed to be right outside the door. When the officer doesn't come, I immediately rise and say you can't come near me and I make my way to the door. I go down the hall to find the officer that was supposed to be guarding me in the room. He is with another officer and he is in his underwear saying he was sorry but he needed to get dressed. Then I woke up.

To me this is a dream about how it is hard for me to trust in law enforcement. They weren't there when I needed them, therefore, in the dream they are not there for me. Knowing this and thinking this are two different things for me. I know when I go into the grand jury room I will be well protected and cared for. One the other hand, the government failed me for eighteen years. And that will take time to heal from.

Raising the Girls in the Backyard

The new baby has just turned two weeks old. I am the mother of two healthy girls. Phillip and Nancy are letting me stay in the studio room with them. Phillip says we can be one big family now. He says he is going to work super hard on the printing business. He wants Nancy to quit her job at CAP to be able to stay home and help with the baby and the business. He says he will get us all the jobs we need.

My days are consumed with the babies and Printing for Less. Since A is three, I am trying to get her to stop nursing. I can't nurse both of them at the same time. Phillip still says I am doing the best thing in the world for the girls. He has told me all the benefits of breast-feeding. I know it's good to breast-feed, but a girl can only do it for so long. A will just have to stop.

The name S just does not suit the baby. We end up calling

her G. She was born with a growth above her eye. It feels like a ball right at the end of her eyebrow. Phillip has felt it and thinks it is nothing but "a cyst." I wish I could have a doctor look at it. Phillip says to continue to watch it and if it starts growing, then he will figure out a way to take her to the doctor. He says maybe one of those free clinics. Nancy could take the baby and it would look like a non-English-speaking Mexican woman taking her baby in for a checkup. Probably with no questions asked. I just hope it doesn't get any bigger so she doesn't have to go to the hospital. I would want to go, too, and I don't think Phillip would allow that.

Phillip has bought a digital camera for the business. He will be gone all day today and I want to use it to take some photos of the baby and A. Nancy gave the baby a really cute dress. It is pink with little flowers on it. I get her dressed and think of the time I was given a disposable camera for pictures of A. Phillip said as long as I took pictures of just the baby he would allow me to take them. Nancy had gotten a really pretty pink dress for the baby at her work. It was crocheted. I got pictures of her walking, taking a bath, and in her favorite rocking chair. When Phillip got them developed for me, I made a scrapbook with them. She was about six months before I was able to get any pictures of her except for one that Nancy took when she was one month old. But I have none from when she was first born. I like having a digital camera because now I can take all the pictures I want and print them right here. G looks so cute as I pose her for a few perfect shots.

Phillip is going out every day to find us jobs. I think Nancy will be able to quit her job soon and spend the whole day with me and the girls. He has set up a CB radio, which we use to communicate with him while he is on the road. On most days he leaves at seven or eight in the morning and doesn't come home until dinnertime around five or six at night. To contact him on the road, he has taught us to say, "Breaker, Breaker, Sky Walker, do you copy?" Sky Walker is his handle. He says we can pick a handle to be called, too, so when he calls we will know it is him and not a stranger on the same frequency. Nancy's handle is Baby Blue. She says Phillip calls her that and when they used to go up to the mountain to get high they would take a CB radio with them and talk to all the truckers. I pick the name Data, which is my favorite character on *Star Trek: TNG,* and A wants to be Tinky Winky from *Teletubbies.* Her favorite show. Phillip says the more time he spends out in the field, the more jobs he can get. The CB radio lets him be out and not worry about us at home.

I can't wait until Nancy can stay home with us all day. I really need some help with them. Phillip is gone most of the day and doesn't help with them when he is home. Yes, I have all I need physically for them, but I wish he would spend some more time at home. I am getting overwhelmed.

A is reminding me more and more of my mom. Sometimes when I look at her all I see is my mom. I must put those thoughts behind me; it just makes me sad to look at her and I don't want to feel that way. I need to change these feelings into something positive instead of negative. Phillip has been teaching me how to use affirmations to change my thinking process. I know in time it will get easier and I won't feel like this every day.

jaycee dugard

Reflection

This seems like a good place to give a little update on how my girls are faring now. It is the first day of real school for them. Wow, I can't believe I am writing those words. This is something I have dreamed about for them for so long. I have done my best to educate them in the backyard, but I could only go so far. My education level only went to the fifth grade.

Phillip always believed school was a terrible environment. He thought it was so much better to homeschool the kids than for them to be in public school. He used to say he had created the perfect environment for raising children. We never had a choice in the matter. Phillip believed public school would expose the girls to bad influences, like bad language, drugs, bullies, and all the things he believed the kids should be sheltered from. While I agree with him that some schools are not the best environment for growing children, I do believe in education. I loved school. I didn't always love the kids that I went to school with—at times they were mean or I was just too shy to stick up for myself—but overall my experience in school was positive. I don't think Phillip enjoyed his school years and that, combined with drug use in high school, gave him a warped sense of what life is like. I believe that in many ways he wanted to create his own little world and for a while he succeeded at the expense of others. I was just a character in his world, a world he created for his own benefit.

My own education stopped at the fifth-grade level and although I have kept myself reading and learning all these years, I still am not a teacher. Thank goodness for the internet! (I know what people are thinking, and the answer is yes—yes, I did think about using the internet to find my mom, but Phillip told me and convinced me that he was monitoring everything I did on the internet and he would find out each and every thing I did on it. He said the computer kept a record of everything and he could see it anytime he wanted.) If not for the internet, I don't think I would have been able to educate the girls at the level I did. When I proposed the idea of enacting an actual school schedule for them, it was at first met with some hesitation. Phillip believed that within a few more years he would be able to hire someone to educate them. The girls also had their own issues with doing school every day; these are very strong-willed girls. Nothing like their mom, or their "sister," as I was known at the time. They didn't understand why all of a sudden they had to keep a schedule. They were used to doing pretty much anything they wanted during the day, as long as it was in the backyard. No playmates for them. No sleepovers. No playdates at the skating rink. Their day was pretty much just video games and certain TV channels and programs approved by Phillip. Anyway, I ended up winning the school battle and before they knew it, I had them going to school from ten a.m. to two p.m. I would print out their worksheets the night before and put them in special folders I made for each of them. They had four subjects—math, spelling/reading, social studies, and science. I loved websites like enchantedlearning.com and www.superteacherworksheets.com, which are great for all subjects. We had a lot of printers. Phillip loved Canon printers and the separate ink cartridges the brand made. It made the printing business a lot cheaper to run because he filled his own cartridges and bought the ink in bulk. So I had everything I needed to print the worksheets for the girls. We always had leftover paper around, so that wasn't a problem either. I would stay up late and print their worksheets at night before I went to bed. In the morning, I would get up at about nine to start my day. I would wake the girls up and tell them to get up and get dressed for the day, then go inside the studio building (now called the office) and make some Hills Bros. Cappuccino, double mocha flavor, while I watched the *Today* show.

The girls would come in and want to go up to the house to get some breakfast. Phillip told them they must always call first. The girls and I grew up knowing he was on parole for the rape of a woman in his past. It wasn't something we questioned him on. Phillip was afraid his parole agent would show up unexpectedly and he didn't want the agent to see where the girls came from. He was sleeping in the house lately with Nancy and his mom. He didn't want anybody to see the back property. I always thought it was so strange that not one of Phillip's parole agents knew that the property extended further back. I just figured they didn't care and thought Phillip was a totally rehabilitated offender. I wanted something to change. I wanted his parole agents to ask questions. If Phillip wouldn't be able to answer, maybe something would change. I also feared whatever change would come. I didn't have anywhere to go. I had the girls to take care of. But I wanted them to have a better life. I just couldn't do it for myself. I needed someone to free me, but no one did.

I, however, have mixed feelings about high school. On the one hand, for eighteen years I had been taught that schools are bad and kids learn bad things there and peer pressure can ruin a child's life forever; but when I consider who I heard all this stuff from, a kidnapper, rapist, pedophile, narcissistic, pervert, I can only come to one conclusion. Maybe school isn't so bad after all! I don't know what my high school experience would have been like. Part of me would like to go back in time and take that first step out of the car as a new freshman, and part of me is so glad I didn't have to. I look at my daughter and see what it could have been like for me had I not been kidnapped and taken away from my life at the age of eleven.

Both of my girls are going to school full-time now. When they first made this decision, I didn't want them to see how the idea scared me to death. How all I could think about was how much school would change them and how lonely I would be without them and how the thought of anything happening to them would just kill me. But I knew saying any of these things aloud wouldn't help. So I supported them. Taking A to shadow at different high schools. Helping G decide what school and grade would be best for her. Taking them back-to-school shopping. And then before I knew it, A's first day arrived. It was a Tuesday. I made her a veggie rollup. I asked how she was feeling, and she said she was nervous and excited. A week before, we attended orientation. What an experience that was. I felt so out of place, like I didn't belong. A nudged me and said, "Hey, you're making me nervous." So after that I really tried to seem calm and in the moment. But all I could think about was if this is what it would have been like for me. That day ended up being really good for her; she was nervous about the other kids, but after seeing that they were just as scared as she was, it helped her to not feel so out of place. Unlike me. I felt very out of place. I think part of it was being afraid people were thinking, How can she be a mom? I'm short and have been told I look very young for my age, and then there's the fact that I gave birth to her when I was fourteen. Of course, people must be curious. Nobody said anything to me, though. And I started to relax and just enjoy being on campus. We listened to the principal. We watched as he introduced his assistant and turned just in time to see her pulling a finger out of her nose! That helped to relieve some of the tension that I felt just from being there. Watching A getting her student ID, gym locker, and watching her interact with the other kids was an eye-opening experience. I realized she's going to be okay. And in realizing that, I have gained peace of mind.

Walking the high school grounds brought up feelings of grief for what I had lost. I even felt some jealousy and envy deep down inside. I should have had the opportunity to have these experiences. But they were forcibly taken away from me. Now I have the opportunity to take back a piece of my life that was taken. I always dreamed about going back to school. Sometimes I even had dreams that Phillip would let me go to school and I would actually dream about my school days. Sometimes they would be so real my mind sees them as actual events.

Early in my captivity I felt so alone. I didn't know where I was, so I didn't believe anyone could find me. I was afraid to try to get away, thinking that even if I could, what if something even worse happened to me? I was so scared. I wonder what would have happened if I was rescued in the very beginning.

I know I'm being redundant and a little off topic here, but Phillip gave me this awful image of the world. To me a large part of the world was made up of pedophiles and rapists. I have come to realize this is not true. There are some really fantastic, wonderful, and helpful people out here who have been amazing and comforting and try every day to do the right thing. I was conditioned to think the outside world was a scary place, and the only place I was safe and my girls were safe was to stay with their dad. He always took care of everything. He always had an answer for everything. If I ever questioned him, yes, he would listen, but then he would tell me why I was wrong and why only his way would work. One of the reasons I stayed was I wanted my kids to be safe. The outside world was scary for me. I was so afraid that if I left or tried to leave and take them both with me, I wouldn't be able to protect them. I knew they were so safe in the backyard; I didn't have to worry about anyone taking them like I was taken.

Being in the outside world at times still scares me, and sometimes I want to hold my kids close and never let go. But I know that I am 1% of the population. Stranger abduction is very rare. I still have to remind myself of this fact every time I drop them off and leave. I hope they grow up with a greater sense of self than I had. I was raised to always be polite to my elders. In most cases this is right, but there are moments in which all of us need to have a backbone and feel that we have the right to say no to adults if we believe they are doing the wrong thing. You must find your voice and not be afraid to speak up. I gave my power to my abductor. I was the one to comfort him when he was the one in the wrong. Where was my comfort? Where was my freedom? Why did I feel the need to comfort my tormentor? Violating my body was not enough? He had to violate my mind as well? He had the ability to turn every situation to suit his needs. What happened to the "bullheaded" part of me? I knew I had to do what he told me and not complain. My fear was doing something wrong and Phillip getting mad and who knows what would have happened then. Instinctively, I knew I had to cooperate with him or else.

I hated what he was doing to me, but I felt helpless to do anything about it. When he would cry afterward and "thank" me for helping him with his sexual problem, I wanted to yell and scream to please let me go. I didn't want to help him with anything. I have come to realize that Phillip Garrido is and was a very selfish man. He took me away from my family. From a mother that I loved with all my soul and I still needed desperately. He did disgusting things to me. He told me all along that I was helping him. He used to cry and say he was sorry, after he was done with me. And I would forgive him and say it was okay, that I was okay. I was not okay! That was the confusing part—he could be an animal doing disgusting things to me one minute and then the next crying and asking for forgiveness. It confused the hell out of me. Now I know it was all a part of his manipulation. A game he has been playing all his life. When he took Katie Callaway, kidnapped and raped her, he used the same excuses he did on me. He had a sex problem he needed help with. He used the same platitudes, such as don't struggle and it will be easier for you. Just let me act out my fantasies and everything will go good for you. Basically the same as what I was hearing.

Even though I have forgiven him, it does not negate the facts. I have learned so many new facts about him, I'm not sure if I have the right to forgive him. I will probably struggle with this question for the rest of my life. Yes, in his mind he wanted us to be a family, but when I think back I can see we were just pretending. Pretending everything was okay. Pretending the girls didn't need to go to school. Pretending that is was normal for me not to be driving. Normal for us to not have friends. Normal that Phillip was hearing voices. He will always be their father. Nothing can change that. There are so many opportunities out there for all of us now. I can't wait to see what the girls do with their lives now there is no one to tell us we can't climb a mountain in Istanbul or fly a plane over the Swiss Alps or even just take a walk by ourselves down a quiet street. All this is open to us now, where once it was not.

It still scares me, the fact that I can't protect my daughters from everything. What mother wouldn't want to protect their child from the dangers of the world? But I have to choose to believe they will both be okay and realize that sometimes when we shelter our children too much, we are really protecting ourselves.

My mom survived the loss of me. I think it was a good thing she had my sister to keep her busy. But she never gave up hope of finding me one day. I know this now. For a long time I chose not to think about certain things like my mom because it was just too painful. Sometimes I would think about "what ifs" or remember certain times we were together, but mostly I just tried not to think at all. I used to only allow myself to think about her on her birthday. I would give myself permission to cry and think about her only then. Sometimes my mind would not cooperate and wander with thoughts of her. Did she stay in Tahoe? Is she thinking of me? One time I got this strange feeling that she was gone from the world. I remember I felt devastated. I had to keep convincing myself that it wasn't true and to stop scaring myself like that. Thank God it wasn't true.

Nancy Becomes "Mom"

Nancy has quit her job at CAP and is staying home now. Phillip says that the printing business is generating enough money to see us through until he becomes famous. He always talks about how one day he will be famous because of the songs he has written. He says he has songs for everyone. He has even written one for his mom. Nancy is always telling me that I need to pump him up, meaning pump his ego so he will continue to move forward and not go back to his old ways. He is taking new medication that his psychiatrist has prescribed him. I have learned that one of his therapists diagnosed him with ADD (attention deficit disorder). He said this therapist changed his life. He finally understands why he felt the need to "self-medicate" all these years. Since they treat ADD with methamphetamines, he believes that's what he subconsciously was trying to do all these years. Now he has been assigned a new psychiatrist who has prescribed Dexedrine for his ADD and Zoloft for his manic depression, which his other therapist also diagnosed him with.

Reflection

What I have learned is the difference between supportive therapy and enabling therapy. In my opinion from reading several
reports and from what Phillip told me I think one of Phillip's
therapists was an "enabling therapist" who explained away why
Phillip didn't show up for appointments. In one incident Phillip
had tested dirty on one of the random drug tests he was asked
to do. When it came back dirty, he told his therapist that he was
at a party and someone must have slipped it in his drink. The
worst part is the therapist apparently believed him and made
excuses to the parole board for him. He and Nancy both saw this
therapist three days before they took me from my home and four
days after. I'm not saying that the therapist should have known;
I'm just saying it's strange that the therapist would not have seen
something amiss. Phillip was given the excuse he had been looking for. His "self-medicating" all these years was apparently due
to the fact that he had ADD and bipolar disorder. The therapist
recommended Zoloft for bipolar and Ritalin for the ADD. I wonder what would have happened if the therapist had held Phillip
accountable?

It's also my opinion that another of Phillip's doctors was also
an "enabler." He used to have Phillip come to his office every
month or so, and apparently he thought Phillip was a changed
man, too. Printing for Less started making and printing his business cards, letterhead, and envelopes. He wanted an exact color
and font match and that was very difficult on ink jet printers and
the color didn't always come out right and we'd have to do a re-
print. In 2008, Phillip went to see him with Nancy. Phillip told

me later when he got home that he had finally told the psychiatrist that he has been hearing voices. Phillip told me that for the next three months the psychiatrist didn't return any of Phillip's messages or letters and that he went without his medication for all those months, too. By then he had switched to Dexedrine for the ADD and wasn't taking anything for the bipolar. Phillip said that with God's help he could control the manic side of his personality. And most of the time he succeeded. Phillip had a hard time focusing on anything for long time periods. His thoughts were scattered, and his mind was going in fifty different directions at once. Everything seemed to be falling apart. We were all miserable. The psychiatrist finally mailed Phillip a prescription for his ADD meds. But what I find strange is: Wasn't this doctor curious as to why his patient was acting like this and what his patient was up to? In my eyes, Phillip was essentially asking for help and didn't get it. What can you say? Then his mom fell and things just got worse.

Phillip says Nancy is really having a hard time when he and the babies call me "Mommy." She says she's had a few miscarriages and her blood pressure problems have always prevented her from keeping a baby to term. That makes me feel really bad for her. Phillip says that she feels like an outsider as she watches me and the kids and it's tearing her apart. He says it would be a good idea to bring us all together so we can all be a family for the kids if we start calling her "Mom" and referring to me as the girls' "sister." I don't want Nancy to feel like she is an outsider. I just don't want to call her "Mom." I have a mom. I love and miss my mom. Doesn't he know how hard this is for me? It would be nice if the girls didn't depend on me for everything. I could use some more help with them, and some adult conversation would be wonderful, too. I know it will be a little confusing for A at first because she is so used to calling me Mommy, but I think she loves Nancy, too, and if she sees me doing it, she'll follow along. If we start now, Phillip says G will think Nancy is her mom and A is young enough to forget about me in time. Nancy will finally feel like part of the family. He says I should pick a name that I like to be called.

After a couple of days of thinking, I decide on my new name and tell Phillip and Nancy my choice. I say I want to be called Allissa. I used to love to watch *Who's the Boss?* and my favorite actress is Alyssa Milano. But I want a different spelling. I want it spelled A-L-L-I-S-S-A. This is what the girls will grow up calling me.

Pretending to Be a Family

It was the Fourth of July yesterday and Phillip wanted us to go up on the roof of the barn and watch the fireworks. I was scared to climb the ladder and even more scared to be up on that old falling-down barn with the girls. But Phillip said it was really sturdy and safe and if it could support him, it could support us. So we all climbed the ladder, and he carried the girls up one at a time. A is four and G is already one and walking everywhere she can. She is always on the go. She is saying words like Lissa, Dada, and Mum.

It is a warm night outside. The stars are shining and the moon is a crescent in the sky above me. I sit on the roof and think of my mom and our competition about the moon. I think of her and sing to myself the song we used to sing together, "I see the moon and the moon sees me, God bless the moon, and God bless me." Miss her so much.

G is getting restless. Nancy is trying to talk to her and get her to watch the fireworks. I think the loud noises are scaring her, and I long to hold her close but I don't want it to look like I'm taking over from Nancy. G is squirming and fighting to get free from Nancy's hold on her. She is reaching back toward me to hold her. I tell Nancy that I will hold her if she wants me to, but she thinks the fireworks are just scaring her. She tells Phillip that she thinks we should go inside. Phillip is getting restless, too, so we all climb back down and go inside, where Nancy gives me the baby to breast-feed. Sometimes I feel like all I do is feed her. She loves to eat, but sometimes I think it is more of a comfort thing with her. She's always so restless and fidgety. She loves her pacifier. We call it her Bucky. I feel better now that she is in my arms. On the roof I felt like my pulse was going to jump out of my skin. I wanted to just grab her and hold her to me. I would not have known what to say to Nancy after that. Our relationship is so tenuous. I am trying hard to hold on to what little we have built.

Phillip and Nancy are taking us to the beach today. I am a little scared because I haven't been out in public for a long time. What if I do something wrong? Phillip says we will just be an ordinary family at the beach. There's nothing to worry about.

When we arrive at the beach, it gives me an amazing feeling of freedom. I know I am not free, though. We park along a rocky cliff and get out to have a look at the ocean. When A gets out she is immediately terrified of the cliff and falls to her knees in fear. I want to go comfort her and tell her it's okay, that there is nothing to be afraid of, but Phillip is there with her instead and tells her he will carry her down.

We spend many hours on the beach. I love playing in the

water with the girls. Nancy comes out to play, too. Phillip sits on the blanket in the sand and reads his Bible. After lunch we all head for a walk down the beach. My legs are burning even though I have been exercising with Nancy. The girls are having a fun day and I'm glad they get to have this experience. Phillip's back starts to hurt him, so we make our way back to the car and go home to the backyard.

A few weeks later, Nancy says she wants us to go get our nails done. She says she is going to work on Phillip to convince him that this would be good for our relationship. On the inside I really don't want to go anywhere. I'm afraid, too. Phillip comes to me and gives me one hundred dollars and says Nancy is going to take me on an outing. He says it will be fun.

I get in the car with Nancy and we take off for the nail salon. I am so nervous. What if the person doing my nails sees my hand shaking? When we arrive, I put on my "I can do this" face and follow Nancy in. She tells the Japanese lady that we want a manicure. I sit down in the chair and hand my hand over to the lady. Thankfully, it is not visibly shaking, but I am on the inside. I just want to go back to the girls. The lady asks me questions and I answer automatically. I am not really here. I am not an actual person. I am nobody. Nobody sees me.

My nails are done and we are back in the car. We stop for lunch at Jack in the Box and eat in the car. Nancy really enjoyed getting her nails done. She got a French manicure and says the lady chipped one of her nails. I tell her I can hardly see it and that her nails look beautiful.

We arrive home. Phillip is sitting in his chair reading the Bible and the kids are watching *The Lion King*. Nothing has changed, yet everything has. I went out today and came back and nobody noticed. Nobody cared to ask who I was.

Our next outing is to Walmart. I stick close to Nancy and feel self-conscious being here. I look no one in the eye. My hands are shaking . . . will anyone notice?

Reflection

I wasn't allowed to leave his "secret backyard" until my youngest daughter was two and we went to the Brentwood Cornfest. By then Phillip had Nancy cut my hair really short and dyed it brown. I had put on about thirty extra pounds from being pregnant and Phillip didn't think there was any way anyone was going to recognize me. I remember being really nervous and when I arrived I stuck real close to Phillip and kept my eyes averted from everyone. Nancy gave me a big baggy black shirt and I wore black jeans. By then I had resigned myself to my fate. The biggest memory I have from that day was, I had no voice and I didn't shout to the world "Hey, it's me, Jaycee!" even though I longed to. I was Allissa, the girl who gave birth to two girls that needed to be protected from the evilness of the world, and that was my main goal. I don't remember too much from that day; I do remember Phillip encouraging me to go on one of the rides. I didn't want to go by myself, but I ended up on the swing ride that takes you round and round. I remember thinking as the ride made circles around itself that I wish I was free like the people I see here. Free to walk around and be me. But I wasn't. The next time we went out was Halloween that same year 1999, we went to the Smith Farm and we all dressed up that year, me and Nancy were hippies, A was Belle from *Beauty and the Beast*, and my youngest daughter was Blue from *Blue's Clues*. Phillip wore his old '70s-style rock 'n' roll outfit that he had kept from his days when he was in a band. He brought his guitar and serenaded anyone that would listen. It was quite embarrassing, but everyone was friendly and polite. The kids got to pick pumpkins and it was fun.

One thing remained the same: I knew we had to return to the "secret backyard," where there was no house to come home to, just a building and by that time a few tents.

One outing melted into the next. I learned to not look people in the eye. I felt if I did, they would ask me questions I couldn't possibly answer. I stuck close to Nancy. I could feel my hands shaking when I reached out to touch something I wanted. In time going out became easier and we even brought the girls shopping with us. But I could never shake the feeling that one day someone would say, "Hey, aren't you that missing girl?" but nobody ever did. I was nobody. Nobody saw me.

Cats

There is a stray cat in the backyard that Phillip feeds and she had a batch of kittens. He calls her "mama kitty." She is going to live in the house with Phillip's mother. He found homes for all the kittens except one who he is keeping tied up in the backyard. He named him Blackjack. He is very friendly. It's nice having a kitty around again. I didn't like how Phillip was treating him, though. When he would go on his "runs," Blackjack could sometimes be heard crying at night. He is not fixed yet, so the crying is loud and gets on Phillip's nerves. To shut him up, he tosses the contents of his urine bucket on poor Blackjack. I hate it and tell him to stop. When he's high on drugs, he never listens to me. But I bring it up again when he's coming off of the drugs and he says he feels bad about doing that to the cat and promises me he won't use that method anymore. I tell him it would help to get him fixed, and Phillip says he will look into getting it done.

Reflection

Blackjack lived a long life. Toward the end I took primary care of him and I was the one that found him when he died. It was very hard for me. At the time, I had made a cat enclosure which he would go in at night to keep safe, and that's where I found him one morning. It was in 2002, he was all curled up dead and stiff. I cried a lot for him. I could tell his time was coming, though, because he was not himself for many days before that.

A few years later, when the girls were little, I used to go outside to be by myself. Sometimes I would feel a pressure build inside of me. The need to run away would feel so heavy that in order to soothe myself, I would sit by myself outside. Not where anyone could see me—just to a point where I felt I was away and by myself. One of my favorite spots was a woodpile that was on the other side of one of the many fences in the backyard. One day I noticed that a stray cat was going back there a lot, so I sat for a long time and watched and, sure enough, out popped three little kittens. I put wet food out for them, trying to lure them out. Only one turned out to be friendly and I asked Phillip if I could keep him and he said yes. The others he took to the local pound for adoption. The one I kept was a male, long hair, he looked like a Maine coon. I named him Tucker. I think he was the first cat that I really felt was mine. Although I loved Eclipse, I never really felt she was mine. I found Tucker myself. I fed him. I made sure he was safe, I loved him deeply. He was always so sweet and affectionate and came whenever I called. Well . . . sometimes. I remember one evening at dinnertime, I called and called and he didn't come for the longest time. I usually let them out during part of the day and then I put them back inside their enclosure at night by feeding them. Well, that day I called and called and was becoming very scared that I would never see him again. When there he comes over the fence and starts meowing for dinner. I was so relieved. He lived in there with a stray cat that we caught in one of those humane cat traps. We kept seeing this black stray cat around the yard and he was eating all the birds, so we decided we needed to do something. We caught him and got him fixed and I decided to keep him, too. I named him Lucky. He turned out to be a very nice cat, too. Very good personality, loved to eat! He lived with Tucker for many, many years. They were like brothers. The day they died broke my heart. To this day, even writing this right now I feel the tears coming.

It all started the day before Halloween. I was in the office, working, when G came running in saying there were two big dogs in our backyard. I became concerned for the kids first of all and ran outside to see them for myself. As soon as I got out there, two big huskies went running back from where they had come from, which happened to be through a hole they had chewed from our neighbors' yard to ours through two fences. I put up a piece of wood and thought that would take care of the problem; looking back, I wish so much I would have taken the time to do a better job of securing that fence, but hindsight is 20-20.

The next day, about midmorning, I was working in the office again, when in came the kids again saying the dogs were back. This time I wasn't as panicky. They seemed harmless to me, and I was sure as soon as I went outside they would go back over the fence. So Phillip, Nancy, the girls, and I went out to the back and shooed them back over and were getting ready to make the hole more secure so it wouldn't happen again. Everyone was out there helping me get the dogs back over and then I turned around and went to say "Hi" to my cats, Tucker and Lucky, but they didn't move because they were dead. I felt such devastation I don't think I moved for a long time. Phillip saw me, then looked at them and saw the huge hole the dogs had made in the enclosure which they were in. The kids were out there, too, and hadn't seen them yet or even realized what had happened, they just saw me sobbing and on my knees. I just couldn't help it. I was so devastated. Phillip stayed with me while Nancy took the girls inside, I'm not sure what she told them, but I stayed outside sobbing. Phillip went over to the neighbors to let them know what happened, and I soon heard them working on the fence. Surely, they could hear me cry, too; but I just wanted them to fix the fence so it didn't happen again to any of our other cats. I cried all day that day and several days thereafter, especially during feeding time when I didn't have to make as many dishes as I used to; those times were especially hard and sometimes I would have A finish. I stayed in bed a lot and slept; the first night I cried so hard during the day that I got a killer sinus headache that night and wasn't able to sleep well. It took time to get over the loss of them, especially Tucker, who I will remember forever because I found him and he loved me.

In 2006, Nancy and I brought home two kittens on one of our thrift store outings for the girls. They were being given away in a box outside of the supermarket. We picked two out and brought them home. The girls named them Princess and Misty. Princess attached herself to my youngest daughter and would

Tucker

Lucky

follow her around like a puppy. Misty was more of the laid-back type and spent many hours in my eldest daughter's lap.

We also had two dogs that used to belong to our neighbor who had months earlier fallen in his house and was moved to an elderly care facility. Phillip brought his two dogs—Mindy, a pit bull/Labrador mix and Rowdy, a German shepherd/rottweiler ball of puppy energy. We soon learned that the two dogs loved to chase cats, and since we had so many on the property, we decided to build a dog run for them. I would take them out once a day for a walk on the leash around the backyard. Rowdy would always pull, so I didn't think anything of it when he suddenly yanked so hard on the leash and tried to pull me toward the old barn that was in the middle of the property. It was half falling down and I warned the girls multiple times to stay away from it. Rowdy was adamant about sniffing around the barn, so I gave in and let him lead me over. There was a small cutout looking into the barn and he immediately jumped up, peered inside, and started whining. I pulled him away and looked in myself and didn't see anything at first because it was so dark in there. I finally saw some movement and discovered it was a tiny kitten. One of the strays in the area had a litter of kittens in our barn. For several days I just watched them and noticed their mother come and go a few times. I took the girls out and showed them from afar the new kittens, and they wanted to bring them in the room. I told them not yet because we really didn't have enough money to take care of four new kittens. I didn't know what to do. All our cats had been fixed, but it was hard to find a program in the area for free or discounted spay or neutering. After the first week I noticed that the kittens were crying a lot and I hadn't seen their mother come back for days. I thought maybe the feral mother became scared and might have abandoned her kittens. After talking with Phillip and letting him know about the kittens, he said we should get them out of the barn and then decide what to do with them. Through that small opening, we were able to wiggle through and pull out the very weak kittens. They looked small and like they hadn't eaten for a while. They had their teeth but appeared younger than I think they actually were. One looked like it had an eye infection and Phillip allowed me to take him to the vet if I pretended to just be his daughter. Whenever I went out, no one seemed to wonder who I was. Phillip would say it was the angels protecting us. I couldn't help but feel I was invisible. The kittens were in good health otherwise and before we knew it they had become part of our growing kitty family.

Unfortunately, when the girls and I were recovered and officers were sent to secure the property, Princess and Misty were not among those rescued; neither was Neo, my gray tabby whom I received on my twenty-third birthday. I feared we would never see the new kittens again either, but fortunately they were in one of the buildings and were able to be caught. It was hard to come to terms with never seeing some of the cats ever again. They were a big focus of our lives and they were family.

I am forever grateful to Officer Beth for keeping an eye on all my cats and finding fosters for them for six months until we were able to reunite with them in January of 2010.

• *Journal Entries* •

In the spring of 1998, I needed an outlet for all the feelings and emotions I was keeping bottled up inside. I knew Phillip would never approve of me writing things down, but I had this compulsion to get some things down on paper. When I was seven or eight, my dream was to be a writer or a veterinarian. I love writing stories and have made many up in my mind over the years. I have tried to instill in my kids a love of reading and even encouraged them to write their own stories. Deciding to share my journal entries was a decision I have thought about long and hard and have come to the conclusion that it is important for me to include my feelings and thoughts during my time in captivity. A lot of them show how much I wanted my freedom, how much I wanted to see my mom, and bring to light my conflicted feelings for Phillip and Nancy Garrido.

MAY 3, 1998

Who am I? At this very moment I don't know. I don't even know who I want to be. I do know who I was. I was a kid who always wanted to be accepted, a part of the crowd. I'm always trying to think of the right thing to say to someone. I wanted to be liked, so I could fit in. When I would start a new school, I had been in 4 different ones by the time I was 11, it was hard for me to be the new kid. Not knowing anyone and playing on the playground by myself was not something I looked forward to, so would always try to find a friend. But I was very shy to do that. They usually made friends with me. In my last school in G. Lake Tahoe at a school called Meyers elementary this one girl came up to me, I was new of course and I was alone on the swings, I remember thinking to myself, Why am I not trying to make friends with the other kids, I hate being alone! But for some reason I just could not go up to a group of kids and ask to play with them, too shy I guess. But anyway to get back to the story; she sits next to me on the other swing and starts talking to me and we become friends, she was very nice. I think she was from Russia or Ukraine, her name was Rowan. Then she introduces me to one of her friends, her name was Shawnee who become my "best friend in Tahoe." She was tall for her age and I was small so I kind of thought of her as my protector. She loved horses and would draw them for me. We had many great days together. And she had a dog named Rowdy who would come on walks with us in the back hills where she lived with her grandma; I loved that dog and was often envious of her because I wanted my own dog so bad. I did have two dogs when I lived with my grandma and grandpa, but the first one they told me they had to get rid of her, her name was Tisha. I cried for days, I remember going outside to go play with her and I couldn't find her, I ran back inside to tell Ninny and Poppy and that's when they told me that they gave her away 'cause she was tearing up the backyard, I was so devastated, looking back I think the worst thing was them not telling me about it and me discovering her all of a sudden gone. After that they took me to Disneyland and bought me a stuffed dog that looked just like her, I slept with that dog every night. I wonder what happened to the stuffed animal.

NOVEMBER 3, 1998

I think I want to live by the ocean one day. Have a little cottage overlooking the ocean. I could walk down the steps right onto the warm sand, hear the waves crashing on the rocks, and watch the seagulls in the clear blue sky.

I miss her. I try so hard to see her face in my mind, but I can't remember. I hate myself for not remembering. Some memories are so blurry it's like a dream or something.

I keep remembering this one time when I was, oh I don't

know, maybe about 7 or 8, anyway I was playing with my best friend, Jessie, and my mom was taking a shower. We decided we wanted to play hide-and-seek. I went into the bathroom and told her* we were going to hide and when she got out of the shower I wanted her to come find us. I guess the shower water was so loud she didn't hear me, but I didn't know at the time and thought she heard me. We hid in the closet. When she came out of the shower and saw that we weren't in the house she must have thought the worst, like someone had taken us because we were gone. I didn't understand her fear at the time. I do now. At the time she was frantic, we were still hiding in the closet we heard her call our names, but I thought she was playing our game, so we stayed hidden. Then I heard her yell and run out the door. When we finally came out she was outside yelling for us and her robe had come undone; she was so hysterical she didn't even notice. When she saw me standing at the door she raced to me and squeezed me tight I thought she would never let me go. I started to cry. I said I was sorry but I thought she had heard me.

DECEMBER 16, 1998

I would give my soul for a picture of her. No, No, No not my soul because nobody can give their soul away . . . can they? I don't know, maybe we share our souls with loved ones throughout our lifetimes. Is that possible? I don't know. Does that kind

---

* When I write "her" I am referring to my mom. Back when I wrote these entries I just could not write the words "my mom"; it was just too painful.

of love exist? I know I feel enormous love every day for my girls. Even though they don't know I'm their mom, I still feel this unseen connection with them. Does she feel the same way about me? Does she know I'm still somewhere out here? I wonder if she knows I miss her. I can't bear to think of her sometimes it's just too painful for me.

DECEMBER 22, 1998

I want things to be different, but I would never change a thing about my life. I would never turn back the clock and change the way things worked out. I love my kids. I wouldn't say I have scars from it, but I do have a few scratches! Like the way I feel about touching. I don't know how I would react to a man touching me after what I have been through. Family touching is different, it doesn't bother me as much when he hugs me anymore. I tell myself he is not touching me in a sexual way; it is more a fatherly way now. Not that I would know what that is like. I want to find love one day. The kind of love I read about, but it sounds so unlucky and unrealistic to hope for that. All Phillip talks about is all the horrible people in the world. I don't think the kind of love I dream about is real. That's okay, though, I still have love in my life from my girls.

MARCH 9, 2002

I want to make myself a better person. The first thing I want to improve is my garden. I've really been neglecting it lately. I don't really know where to begin. I haven't been very good at following through lately. I just cannot find the motivation I need. That is another thing I would like to change.

JUNE 2, 2002

I miss her. I wonder what she thinks about. I wonder if she ever thinks about me. Sometimes I hope that she doesn't because I don't want her to be sad and sometimes I wonder if she is happier that I'm not around anymore. I don't like that thought!

I have all these memories; some are cloudy, but they are all there in my head. I think at first I tried to shut down all the memories that are fuzzy for me now. I remember one time he ["he" means Phillip, I tried to leave out names in case Phillip ever read it] was asleep and I was sitting next to him and I felt like I was reliving the time I spent with my aunt and uncle and their kids, my cousins. The memories were so vivid I must have sat there for hours waiting for him to wake up just thinking of my old life. I don't know why I thought back to that moment, time in my life. Maybe because that was another time in my life I felt as lonely as I do now. It was hard being away from her. No one would listen when I said I didn't want to stay there. It's not that my aunt didn't want me there. I felt I didn't belong with them. I felt like an outsider, I wanted to go home!

Does she miss me?

JULY 16, 2002

What is the difference between the heart and the soul? I think there's a big difference. My heart is an organ in my body.

My soul is me. People in my life have helped my soul grow and continue to grow. So many people do not listen to their soul. I know it's just a word, but that's how we have learned to communicate; with words and through behavior. It's only human to use words to describe what can never be touched. My cats, Tucker, Lucky, and Blackjack share a hold on my soul. I love them with my soul. That sounds silly as I write it but it's what I feel for them. They make me happy and mad sometimes at the same time. Blackjack is playful and faithful. Tucker is too curious for his own good; he is also too lovable for his own good. Lucky is . . . well, I don't quite know how to describe him. When he wants to be scratched, but when I go to scratch him he backs away. I understand he must have had a hard life as a stray before he came to live with me. I know he likes me because he sticks around even though he could leave anytime. I know he stays 'cause I feed him but I feel deep down it's more than that. I love it when they all follow me around; it makes me feel good. I can't describe the feeling for some reason, but I do feel important, like they actually want to be with me. Boy, that sounds really silly. I need to do more for them.

AUGUST 22, 2002

I'm sitting here wanting to write so many things, but I don't know where to begin. I cried a little last night. Not a lot, just a little. I was just feeling terrible. Sometimes I want to run away from everything. I would live in my own world. I would have super powers. Like the power to heal people and animals. I would also be able to hear the thoughts of animals and people, too. I would be able to understand animals. I would travel around my world on a horse the color of fire with a mane of snow. I would be a heroine in my world. I would travel everywhere helping people along the way with their problems and there would be only happiness in my wake. Perhaps I would meet my soul mate on one of my journeys and we would continue the journey together. Before the journey ended we would have to find some kind of evil and conquer it together and live happily ever after. Boy, if only I could live in my mind. I know I would never run away. I love the girls too much to ever leave them. We either go together or not at all. So for now it's not at all.

SEPTEMBER 30, 2002

I want things to change. Maybe first I need to change myself. I will never stop exercising. I want to be physically fit and mentally fit as well. Sometimes I wish I could go back to school to learn more. I know I'm learning things here from him. From being a part of this, but at times I feel weak like I can't do anything. I don't have any skills. I would love to be a writer someday. I love to write. I have no idea what I would write about. I like reading fairy tales and mythology. And I also love romance novels. Not the gross sexual ones but the ones about finding the perfect person for you. I like the thought of that one person out there searching all their lives for one person who makes them feel complete like Nora Roberts novels and Danielle Steel. I like Nora Roberts more because they feel more real. No, real is not the right word because the stories aren't really real. Life is not kind to all of us.

OCTOBER 2, 2002

I said I would not leave them; I know I won't because I'm a coward! I've always been a coward. I get so nervous when unexpected things happen I feel helpless, scared, and my face feels like a mask and it betrays my feelings. My chin quivers when I'm nervous or upset. I hate it my hands even shake. They seem to shake all the time; I can't control them either. I'm not afraid. Not when I'm home, it's when I'm out with Nancy and around people I get so scared. Do they see me?

DECEMBER 16, 2002

I want to feel whole. Will I ever feel complete? Love, Justice, Wisdom, he says these words are the keys to life. Do I have these things? I have safe love. Justice? Do I have Justice for what happened?

JANUARY 4, 2003

One time I had this thought that when we have the money and he gets going with his music or whatever that I would search the world for top teachers, psychologists, and doctors and I would be behind the scenes. I would organize and we would open a free clinic for homeless people to come and interact with animals. Animals bring so much comfort to me, I think they would fill a place in the homeless people's hearts, too. The clinic would help these people get back on their feet and feel better about themselves. I don't know exactly how it would work, but I saw this ad in a magazine maybe they could help: Lisa and Gray Silverglat owners of M'Shoogy's Emergency Animal Rescue: 11519 State Rte. C., Savannah, MO 64485.

JANUARY 31, 2003

Please, please stop these restless feelings. I can't stop myself from imagining me just taking the girls and getting in the car, starting it, and leaving this horrible place forever. I know I can't leave. I tell myself that every day. But I want to be away from here so bad it consumes me. Where would I go? Who would help me? Could I find a job? Would he come after us? I know there is nowhere to go. These thoughts and feelings need to be squashed. Things will get better. I have to keep telling myself this. I don't even know how to drive, but I can still see myself doing it just to get away. Please, please stop.

FEBRUARY 22, 2003

I want to be more independent. But how? I don't think I could survive by myself outside of these walls. I wouldn't know how to take care of myself or the kids. The world is so messed up. Why do people ruin their lives? The answers seem so simple to me sometimes and sometimes I see how complicated the answers are, too. Why do I have to miss her [my mom] so much? She hasn't been a part of my life in so long. I don't even remember what she looks like. Would I even recognize her if I saw her? Do people have connections like that? Would my soul recognize hers? I don't know. I hope I get the chance to find out one day.

Sometimes I dream about her. They are fuzzy, hazy dreams; I don't even remember them that well when I wake up, I just know she was in them. My last memory is of her forgetting to kiss me good-bye that morning. I was mad because I asked her the night before to kiss me good-bye before she went to work. She forgets. When I was walking around the track that Nancy has set up in the backyard to exercise with, I thought about her so much I started to cry.

MARCH 11, 2003

Instead of the clinic that I mentioned setting up before, I think it would be more like housing instead. Maybe on a ranch with horses and all sorts of other animals. We could find jobs for everyone that needed one around the ranch and then they wouldn't be homeless anymore. I don't know that much about running a ranch like that, but I intend to learn. Maybe one day it would be a big community of people. I really want a ranch one day with horses. I want to take in all the injured and unwanted animals. They would all have a place on the ranch. And in return those animals would give the people on the ranch a sense of worth.

APRIL 4, 2003

Dreams. Are dreams real or are they made up from memories and things that happen during the day? I don't really know. I hope they are just dreams. Things that will never really happen like that. I never really have nightmares, only once in a while. A few years ago I had a dream about my grandpa, Poppy. I dreamed he was in his truck [he was a truck driver] and he had a heart attack and tried to cross the road and got ran over. That's why I hope dreams are just dreams and not real. Sometimes I want to stay in my dreams when she [my mom] is in them. Just hold on to them for a little bit longer to be with her again if only it's for a few minutes, but I always wake up. Some of my dreams are weird, like in one I'm trying to open my eyes but I can't, but that's when I know I'm dreaming.

MAY 3, 2003

I felt lonely all day today. I don't understand why I feel like this sometimes. I mean it's not like I'm alone. I have my family and they are great. I don't really know why I feel like this. I just want a chance to do things myself. Lead a life that I choose not this life that I have no say in what happens. No real control. What do I want? Maybe to feel a little more grown up. I feel sometimes like I'm still the same age as when IT happened. I hate this feeling. I want to grow up. But how do I do that here? Who would I be if I weren't here? Sometimes I think I would be a totally different person because being here has changed me. I might have always followed in someone else's footsteps. Always trying to get people to like me. Always wanting nobody to be mad at me. Oh who am I kidding, I'm still that same person. Well maybe not as much as before. I have changed. I know now I would not follow the leader of the pack blindly, I would not do drugs or break the law. I wish I had better instincts, though.

JUNE 6, 2003

Reading is an escape for me. I ask myself, what am I escaping from? I don't know, I just . . . maybe I am escaping myself. I'm not happy or comfortable with myself. When I'm reading I can lose myself, maybe even become like the beautiful women I read about. Strong, independent women that do things by themselves. I should be taking control of my body and getting strong and healthy; I put on so much weight from the babies, my body has changed so much. I just can't seem to get motivated. I just can't say no to food! She [Nancy] is always bringing in so much candy and, yes, I love it, but it does not help my weight. I just can't say no to her [Nancy]. Maybe one day when I'm finally ready to take control of myself I will.

AUGUST 11, 2003

My cat Blackjack died on this day; I wrote this in memorial to him.

Why do we allow ourselves to love when we know for a fact that, that soul will eventually leave us??? I will miss him. There are no words that offer comfort, but to not write anything at all feels wrong. Hearts become attached as easily as they become broken and our minds are left sifting through the pieces, which I fear take a lifetime to put back together to achieve any form of acceptance. I will always love him.

AUGUST 21, 2003

Life moves so fast. It has been a while since I last wrote and I feel different and the same. Sometimes all I can think about is the way I look. I feel ugly because I'm fat and my face is so awful, full of pimples. I try so hard to . . . to what? Why do I care what I look like? My family loves me just the way I am, they are the only ones who see me, so what do I care? But I want to be pretty, not gorgeous, just pretty. I want a healthy body and flawless skin. Am I vain? It makes me depressed the way I look now. I hate mirrors, but I also want a mirror to see myself. To see if all the exercising I am doing with Nancy is paying off. Why is it important to me? I tell myself that I am going to have to face the way I look because why dwell on it when I'm doing all I can to better myself, what more can I ask of myself. I hate feeling down. I want to be happy.

SEPTEMBER 2, 2003

I don't understand why I'm not happy. I am happy . . . I mean I should be happy. I have a lot more than other people do. I just feel angry that I will never see my friend again [Jessie] or my real family. I guess in a way I never really knew them; I really didn't even know her [my mom], maybe that's what's eating at me . . . I'm afraid I'll never really get the chance to know her [my mom]. What if something happens to her [my mom]. Life is so uncontrollable. It just continues and we just ride the wave it creates. Sometimes I want to lead my own life. But why? It would be in my best interest to stay and go with this flow. I read stories of adventure and true love and, yes, I want it, everyone wants that—

look at all the books written about those subjects! I want to find it, but I don't think it really truly exists or ever happens. It's just dreams people have and wish for to make life more worthwhile in this dangerous would we live in. Something to keep their hearts from shattering. I don't think it really happens, though, I have never seen it. I don't think I will find it either. I will live my days alone because I will not settle for anything less than true feelings.

OCTOBER 12, 2003

I guess I have turned a switch off inside of me. In the beginning I did it to survive. Now it's just habit, I suppose, but nonetheless it is now a part of who I am. I feel it switch when I watch TV or I'm out somewhere. When I'm out in public I want nothing more than to be invisible. To blend in and not get noticed. That's when I feel the switch turn on and me sink into the background. I don't look at people or really see them either. I feel like if I notice them, they will notice me. I want to have a normal life and be like normal people, but I can't, the switch always turns on. I'm also afraid if I see people, I'm afraid of what I would see. It's not that I don't care, I care! I care more than I want to. I just can't stand crying over any of it anymore maybe because I've done enough crying for two lifetimes. I can't say, though, that people don't affect me; I would be lying to myself. I want to change the world, make it a better place to live. A place where I want the kids to live in.

NOVEMBER 8, 2003

[*Journal entry about a kitten that I named Precious that I found outside, but she was very sick and ended up dying.*]

Oh God, I feel awful. I hurt so badly. Why do I feel this way? I only knew her for a short time. I think this is the first time someone I loved has died. I know I've lost many people in my life that I have loved even more, but this is the first one that has died in my arms. I know people would think I'm crazy for crying over her because she was just an animal. Sometimes I feel more connected with them than I could ever feel for a human being. Is that weird? I will never forget her [Precious]. How could she have gotten lodged in my heart so quickly?

NOVEMBER 9, 2003

I feel scared right now. I'm thinking what if I never get to see her again. What if she dies! I would never really get to know her and there is nothing I can do about it. I'm helpless. I feel better after I write down what I'm feeling. I don't really have anyone to share them with. I don't think they [Phillip or Nancy] would even really want to hear what I'm thinking. I don't want to make them sad with what I'm feeling anyways. They don't ask me a lot, so it's not hard to keep all my junk inside. I've heard the expression "time heals all wounds." One day I hope to understand what that truly feels like.

DECEMBER 18, 2003

On a promo for the news tonight the press is speculating that the man that killed Polly Klass also took and killed me. It is so hard to express the feelings I'm feeling. They showed a brief picture of me and then the killer. That was so painful to watch. Phillip thinks it would be a bad idea for me to watch the news tonight; I think he's right, I'm not going to watch it. I wonder if they will show a picture of her [my mom]. I hope they don't bring it all up for her again. Why can't they just leave it in the past? I hope they don't hurt her. What must she be thinking? Does she think I'm dead? I miss her more than I can understand. Sometimes I'm afraid I won't recognize her. Sometimes I wonder if I was ever given the choice, would I stay here or leave? There is no easy answer. There is a piece of me missing. Part of me will always be there with her [my mom], there is a part of me that always hurts and feels the pain of losing my family and that part wants to become whole but that cannot happen until I am united with those I lost. I wish I was stronger.

Affirmations:

1. Only I can make it happen.
2. I control what I eat.
3. Every day I become the person I want to be.
4. I have the strength to do everything I set my mind to.

DECEMBER 30, 2003

There are times I forget who I am. Tonight I have so many memories running through my head, good and bad. Time and separation dulls some of the memories, but the essence is always there with me every day. One day when I see her again maybe the pain will go away. I know I'm not the first person to lose someone they love and I most certainly won't be the last. I'm probably considered lucky, if you can call it that, because I know I will see her again one day; not everyone can say that.

I know this may sound silly but not easy. Imagine somebody's life going on after you leave; you only focus on your life and its events. So now I wonder what kind of life has she had? I'm thankful and I hope she is, too, that she has my sister with her. As I'm writing this she is twelve. Wow, I can't ever begin to guess what she's like. I wonder what they do together? I hope they are happy as I am most times. I wonder if she asks about me and what she tells her. I have no clue what I would say under these circumstances. I guess I'm the lucky one in my knowledge that I will see them again one day. It brings me a lot of comfort just to say or write those words.

DECEMBER 31, 2003

Here I am sitting in my room [tent] thinking where will I be in the future on this same day in this same hour? What is going to change in the New Year? The one event that sticks out is Blackjack's death. I will remember him forever. Another thing that was good about this year was getting Neo. That changed my world for the better. But looking back over the year, so little has changed from the previous year. We are stuck in a bubble. My hope is that this year will be full of change. I want to do so many things. I feel I will never be able or given the chance to do what I want to do. In my mind he [Phillip] is making everything more complicated than it needs to be, but maybe I see it that way because my mind is simple. I prefer my life simple and uncomplicated because I know his situation is anything but simple.

FEBRUARY 3, 2004

Why does it always have to be something holding us back? It's like we have to fight for each step we take in our lives never knowing exactly where it will lead us, but fighting nonetheless! Why does he [Phillip] make a simple sentence seem so complicated? When will life feel like living for? I wish it was now, I'm so tired! Tired of being not in control of my life because it is my LIFE! Why do people think they have the right to my life?

10 things that make me Happy

1. Hearing someone laugh
2. When my cats are near me
3. Birds singing
4. When animals like me
5. Blue skies and puffy clouds
6. The rain
7. Having something fun to do
8. The ocean

9. When someone says something kind to me
10. Knowing someone loves me

FEBRUARY 7, 2004

I'm sitting and thinking it's so hard to change habits. I'm trying to write out a plan for my future, but it's hard. I feel I have no future. I thought it would be easier. It's the New Year and by the end of it I plan on making changes in myself. It's a slow process (changing) but everything counts on me making these changes, I feel like the world depends on it. I know that sounds really egotistical but I feel it.

I remember having a dream a few years ago about my grandpa. In the dream I saw my grandpa's truck [he was a truck driver] at what looked like a shopping center parking lot and he was lying in his truck. I think he was dead. It looked like he had been beaten.

[*I later found out when I was reunited with my mom, that my grandpa was hit by a car and killed.*]

MARCH 13, 2004

I'm sorry. Sorry for everything I can't be. Sorry I can't be what he wants me to be. I don't even know exactly what that is. I'm just sorry. Sometimes I feel so alone, I know that's crazy because I'm not alone. I have my cats and people who love me, too. It's just I don't know what I want. Some days I can clearly see everything and things seem easy, and the next day seems blurry and I can't see what I want. Nights are the worst because I have too much time to think. Sometimes I think I'm being too dramatic and complain too much. What do I have to complain about? I have food, I have shelter from the rain, well, unless my tent is leaking. I don't want to hurt him [Phillip]; sometimes I think my very presence hurts him. So how can I ever tell him how I want to be FREE to come and go as I please? FREE to say, I have a family. FREE.

MAY 23, 2004

I usually don't write about my day-to-day life, but today was just so horrible I had to get it down on paper. The day started out bad. Phillip was in a really bad mood and you could tell early on in the day that all he was going to get done was sleep on the couch all day. I hate it when he is so lazy. While I work all day, he gets to do anything he wants. I am so tired of that, but I can't do anything about it. Nancy had already asked him the day before if she could take me thrift store shopping and he said yes. Sometimes I like going out with Nancy and sometimes I do not. She can be so cold, and it makes me feel like I have done something wrong. She asks me where I want to go, but then when I tell her, it's like I've made the wrong decision, so I've learned to try to feel her out ahead of time so I know the right answer. Today we headed to the Goodwill in Pittsburg, and then the Salvation Army in Antioch. I always show her the clothes I would like to buy to see if she likes them, too. When we came to the shoes, I sat my purse down on the chair while I tried on a pair of shoes Nancy said I would like. After I tried them on and discovered they were too big, I put them back on the shelf and followed her to another aisle. A minute or two later I realized I forgot my purse and told Nancy I had to go back to the shoe aisle. When we went back and looked around, my purse was nowhere to be found. It had been stolen. I was in disbelief for a minute. Stunned. I felt like a part of me had been stolen. I know it's irrational, but that's how I felt. I felt stupid and apologized to Nancy for my careless-ness. She had given me the money for the PG&E bill and I put it in my purse for safekeeping and now it was gone. I felt shaky and ready to cry. I walked over to the little kids' section while Nancy placed a call to Phillip. I sat down in one of the little chairs for the kids to use while their mothers shopped and cried. I don't know why I was crying. I knew I could easily work off the stolen money. It was more than that. I felt like I never wanted to leave "home" again. I couldn't believe someone would steal my belong-ings. I feel like it is not safe to leave this place. I feel it is not safe to leave the safety of Phillip's backyard. At least I know what to expect here.

JUNE 27, 2004

Lonely, that's how I feel. Lonely and incomplete. I want to run but have no idea where to run to. I want to yell, but I don't want to hurt anybody. I want to say something, but I don't know what to say. Love is the easy part; it's the living without the love you need that is hard.

Is life worth living simply because you live, or is it worth more if you make life happen? What if you have no choice in the matter? Maybe you have to make life happen whether it is good or bad; you make the choices in your life and have to live with the consequences of your choices. Did I have a choice "that day"? Could I have chosen to stay home from school? I would have been punished, but my life would not have changed so completely as it did. Would I choose to be here even with everything's that happened?

JULY 5, 2004

It feels like I'm sinking. I'm afraid I want control of my life. This is supposed to be my life to do with what I like, but once again he [Phillip] has taken it away. How many times is he allowed to take it away from me? I'm afraid he doesn't see how the thing he says makes me a prisoner. Does he want to see it?

I've been thinking of her a lot lately. I know it would take just a couple of clicks, I could see her. I need to see her. So, what's stopping me? I think I'm afraid to take the first step because I know I could not go any farther with it. And that would hurt me. I'm such a coward! I hate being afraid. Why don't I have control of *my life*! I feel now I can't even be sure my thoughts are my own. I can't even really talk to him [Phillip] about anything I feel because he will just think the angels are controlling me. I don't want to burden him with what I'm feeling. Why should I even care if I hurt him, he has hurt me! I just can't do it back. I can't be like them.

SEPTEMBER 4, 2004

I'm just surging with anger right now. I can't help it. I think what he did is wrong. Why couldn't he just once give in and not be so controlling! It helps to write these feelings down. I can't talk to him. He overpowers me with his words in no time. Then there's the fact that I can't put what I'm trying to say in the right way. What I want to say never comes out the way I envision it in my head. Why is that? I wonder if I could have prevented the fight by going out there myself, then again maybe he would have told me the same things. If I told him any of my feelings he would immediately tell me "the angels are controlling you." I need him to give me the freedom to talk to him, but right now that's not going to happen. So I will just let these feelings flow through me and out this pencil. It's weird, but I already feel the tension leaving me and soon I will only be left with the memory of this night to think about and analyze, rethink, and come to a conclusion about what to do. Maybe the tension is leaving me because I'm no longer around him; I'm out here in my own space. I love my tent! It's my own space to do with as I wish. As soon as I see him again, all I want to do is tell him how wrong he was to do that. But he will never take responsibility for what he does. It's always someone else's fault, the angels now mostly. If I confronted him, he would just think I'm being controlled to say these things by the angels and that would get me nowhere. Sometimes I wish I could live very far away from him [Phillip]; sometimes I dream about it.

OCTOBER 3, 2004

Sometimes I think the memories from what he did to me would fade more quickly if I didn't have to see him every day 24/7. It's hard. And I hate the memories from that time. I want them to go away forever. I miss her. I would give anything if she could just hold me one more time. Would she let me go again? It's nights like this I wish for someone to hold me safe. Neo is here and he brings me comfort, I don't know what I would do if I didn't have him with me.

10 things I want to do

1. Lose weight
2. Do yoga in the morning
3. Write more
4. Learn something new
5. See all the people I care about
6. Learn 2 different languages
7. Learn to paraglide
8. Travel around the world
9. Learn to snorkel
10. See my mom

MARCH 28, 2006

My Dreams for the Future

1. See Mom
2. See Pyramids
3. Ride in a hot-air balloon
4. Learn to drive
5. Swim with dolphins
6. Touch a whale
7. Take a train ride
8. Learn to sail an old-fashioned sailing ship
9. Write a best seller
10. Horseback ride on the beach every day

This is one of the Bible studies Phillip made us sit through:
John 1:1

Wisdom was created before everything.

God represents a way of living one's life. God holds and stands by wisdom, love, and justice. They are one.

[The]woman is in all of us. She represents our subconscious. She is inside of us always making good and bad decisions. Man represents male and female. The garden or field in the Bible is the inner workings of our minds. God developed man [humans, male and female] through stages in the evolution of our minds. We as humans have not yet awakened from the deep sleep and we have not become one with our inner woman [subconscious]. We have not shed our clothes [bad behavior] and become naked. Living as God [a way of life] our creator intended.

The serpent in the Garden of Eden [our minds] represents our subconscious and our conscious talking to each other. Like the battle sometimes we have within ourselves. Telling us to do something even when you know it's wrong or has the potential to be wrong or dangerous if you have never had the experience of doing it, how can you ever win the battle? So the woman [Eve in the garden, our subconscious] gave the apple [a new experience] to her husband [our subconscious, Adam]. Our creator knew the only way to develop man so he could one day become like God was to let man learn through experience.

The breath of life our creator breathed into all was the freedom to make choices, good and bad. That's why he gave us a helper [our subconscious, our inner woman] to be with us through our journey of learning.

From the very beginning we have struggled with the way of

God and our minds. The story of Cain and Abel represents the turmoil with us. Cain is the negative input we encounter every day and the consequences of letting those thoughts take over. Abel is what we know is right but don't always listen to. And when we let Cain [the negative] win, we kill Abel [our sense of what's right]. But as with all aspects of our life, we have the ability to change and grow and learn from our mistakes. Our inner woman can be good or bad depending on the choices we make in life.

MAY 16, 2006

Favorite Song/Artists

Kelly Clarkson: Behind These Hazel Eyes, Miss
  Independent, Walk Away
3 Doors Down: Superman Kryptonite, Close to Home
KT Tunstal: Black Horse & the Cherry Tree
Maroon 5
Matchbox 20
Dido: White Flag
Nickleback
Green Day: Boulevard of Broken Dreams
One Republic
5 for Fighting
Jason Mraz: The Remedy

SEPTEMBER 18, 2006

Had a breakdown today. They [the angels] used him to hurt me. Unacceptable! He cut me deep inside, deep damage done will take time to repair. At first all the anger was directed at both of them [Phillip and Nancy], but time makes things clear and blame is in the right place now. I know I will get over it. Love will prevail. I will win!

SEPTEMBER 20, 2006

Found out that he took money from us again. He says the angels made him do it. He never takes responsibility for anything. Even though last time he said it wouldn't happen again. He still did it. They [the angels] want me to hate him [Phillip] for doing this to us again. I know I shouldn't blame him, but it's hard not to. He wants me to believe the angels made him do it and it's not his fault. I know in his mind he took the money for a good reason, not intentionally to hurt us but still. I wanted to scream and yell at him like he did to me. I didn't! I can't count on him for anything. It's hard to not be angry with him. I need to work on that. He also yelled at A and made her cry, which he also blamed on the angels.

SEPTEMBER 21, 2006

All Phillip and Nancy do is sleep all day. They want me to think it's the angels doing it, but when will they start trying to help themselves? I work all day and they sleep. It ridiculous!

They were going to tell the psychiatrist about the angels today and how Phillip hears voices, but Phillip says the angels made both him and Nancy so sleepy that they couldn't drive and tell the doctor. They still went today and all seemed to go okay. Maybe he will get the help he needs now from the psychiatrist.

SEPTEMBER 27, 2006

Felt sad all day today. I feel like everything is hopeless.

NOVEMBER 5, 2006

The angels gave Nancy suicidal thoughts today. Very hard to hear her talking like that. Gives me feelings of hopelessness.

FEBRUARY 21, 2007

I have feelings of hopelessness. I feel like nobody cares. This year has been extremely hard. First, it feels like we aren't getting anywhere. One of our clients that witnessed Phillip doing his "Can you hear me?" backed out today and took back her signature. Phillip says it's because the angels worked with her husband and that made her take back her witness. It makes me feel like everyone who believes is going to abandon us. Recently Phillip told us he has been untruthful about the money we make again and he was using it to buy stuff. He wouldn't tell me what. It makes me feel like I can't trust him. He says that's what the angels want. To turn us against each other. It's so confusing.

I've had a few bad dreams lately, too . . . nothing like before, though. One was about a serial killer coming and killing us all and nobody would ever know.

Phillip says the angels give him terrible dreams, too, he says they make him feel dirty. Nancy has been having a terrible time, too. Lots of bad dreams that Phillip says the angels torture her with.

Sometimes I don't want to live on a planet that lets such horrible things happen. I will not give up, though.

MARCH 16, 2007

I've been feeling very pressured lately. It feels like everything is riding on me doing something. Like when "Can you hear me?" was riding on me hearing it and I could never hear it. Now it's either send the emails to people who hear voices and people of the church or nothing is going to happen. Why does he put so much pressure on me? Why can't he make his project happen? I have enough work to do just to keep us surviving.

Affirmation to counteract the negative feelings I have inside.

1. I am a creative, positive, successful, and happy person.
2. I can achieve anything I set my mind on.
3. We will succeed in everything we are trying to accomplish.
4. I am a strong and capable person.
5. We will succeed.
6. I will have a strong and healthy body and mind.
7. Anything and everything is possible with love.

8. Our goals are attainable.

9. It's easy for me to get up every day and exercise.

10. It's easy for me to eat healthy.

11. I make it a habit to be happy.

12. I will be more assertive.

13. Today is a glorious day.

14. Every day I work toward my goals.

15. I make every day a positive day.

Favorite Quotes: May 1, 2007

The world turns and the world changes, but one thing does not change. However you disguise it, this thing does not change: the perpetual struggle of Good and Evil.

—T. S. Eliot

What will happen will happen. There is time for miracles until there is no more time, but time has no end.

—Dean Koontz

Hope, love, and faith are all in the waiting.

—Dean Koontz

I said to my soul, be still and wait without hope; for hope would be hope for the wrong thing.

—T. S. Eliot

Places I will go one day

1. Egypt
2. Victoria Falls in Africa
3. Alaska to see the northern lights
4. Norway to see Aurora Borealis
5. Italy
6. Greece
7. Ireland
8. Galapagos Islands

Surviving

Pat has become very ill. Phillip lets the girls stay in the house with her to keep her company. The other night she fell and the girls called Phillip and he called an ambulance. She was taken to the hospital and diagnosed with Parkinson's and low-grade dementia. Nancy, myself, and the girls are pitching in to take care of her, which is turning out to not be easy. She is losing her ability to walk and cannot go to the bathroom by herself. I am allowed in the main front house to take my shift with her. Nancy has started sleeping in the house to be near her at night, and the girls are sleeping in the blue building which I have always called "next door." I am sleeping in my tent out back.

Every few years I get a new tent because tents don't last forever. This one is going to last me a little longer than the others because a month prior to putting it up, Phillip had built an elevated floor for it and it helps to keep it dry. Phillip is sleeping in the house on the couch or in the spare room with Nancy. A new law has been enacted and he is being seen quite a bit by his parole officer. It makes it harder to go on outings now.

A few months later, Phillip was suddenly informed that he has another new parole officer and needs to report in. When his parole agent would come over in the beginning, Phillip would tell us that we needed to stay in the back. Eventually he started to get mad at the system and didn't care if we were in the house or not. He now lets the kids sleep in the house. One time a parole agent paid a surprise visit on Phillip and saw one of the girls sleeping in one of the spare rooms. I was told of this later by the girls because they were scared. Phillip told me the next time a parole agent came to the house, I was to ask if he was the one that went into my daughter's room.

After that Phillip was informed he was getting yet another new parole officer. One day when I was in the house taking care of his mother, this new parole agent came and I asked him if he was the agent who walked into my daughter's bedroom. He answered no and I proceeded to wheel Pat back to her room. He took Phillip's urine sample and left. More and more frequent visits are occurring at the house, and Phillip is becoming more and more frustrated and paranoid. In his mind he is doing nothing wrong. It's preventing him from doing this effectively with all the monitoring. He wants to get a lawyer and get off of parole.

There is a washer and dryer in the house, but the dryer doesn't work and neither does the washer, but we desperately need a washer. The printing business is not doing so well and we don't have a lot of money, especially for going to the Laundromat and washing clothes. Phillip has finally fixed the washer. In order to use it, though, it has to be outside because the drainage in the house is not working. So we moved the washer outside. It was incredibly heavy and took all of our strength to move it out to the middle of the yard under a pine tree. Once he got it all hooked up, it was so nice being able to do the laundry and not waiting for it to pile up on us. Especially since Pat has gotten sick and has had a lot of bed wetting and pooping accidents and we would have to wash her sheets a lot.

It seems like the house has started to fall apart since Pat got sick. Nancy found a huge water puddle in the middle of the house and when Phillip went under to check it out discovered the pipes were rotting. The downstairs porch sink was always backed up with water and Phillip has showed us how to drain it with a siphon hose. It has to be done at least three times a day or the sink tub will overflow and then we'd have to clean up the floor. It's already happened a few times and is a pain to soak up all the water on the floor. The water that backs up from the drain is black and gray—it's so disgusting! I hate the job of draining. But I hate my shift with his mom even more. She is getting really demented and the only one she is nice to is her darling son who could never do anything wrong. She says really mean things when I have to take her to the bathroom or walk her or exercise her. She hates everything except Phillip. Nancy has a hard time with her, too, but sometimes can get her to listen. I feel like she deep down hates me, though, and knows what I represent even though we have never told her, I think she knows I represent a side of her son that she doesn't want to acknowledge exists.

Before she fell I had only seen her a couple of times. She knew me as Allissa, the sister of the girls that Nancy brought over from down the street, which was the story that Phillip told her. Sometimes I think he would say these are your grandkids, too. I'm not sure what she thought. She didn't do much after she retired; just watched TV all day and sometimes went shopping with her sister Celia, the one Phillip gave my cat to. After Pat's fall, Celia died and Nancy had to tell her. Some days she remembered and others she didn't. The Parkinson's was eating her body and the dementia was eating her mind. It's a sad thing. Maybe it's better that she will never truly know that her son did such an evil thing.

Discovery and Reunion

On August 24th, Phillip took the girls to the FBI office in San Francisco. He said that he liked to take the girls with him because he thought that people were more apt to listen when they were with him. I thought that at least it gave the girls a chance to get out of the house for a little bit. We had not been able to go anywhere during that year because we had to take care of Pat and she couldn't be left home alone for long. The advanced stages of Parkinson's and dementia were taking a toll on her.

When Phillip and the girls returned home later that afternoon, everything seemed normal. I asked how it went and if everything went the way he wanted it to. And he said he had met two cops from the Berkeley campus who were very interested in what he presented. He said "they flipped" (a term he used often when describing people's reactions) and were excited to hear more about his discovery, which was that others could hear him speaking with the power of his mind with the aid of his "black box." He also dropped off his documents entitled "Schizophrenia Revealed" to the FBI office in San Francisco that day, too. He said he was met with similar reactions. According to Phillip, this was it and he was finally going to be able to move forward with his "God's Desire" church and "fight for God." I really didn't think too much about what he said that day because I had heard it countless times before. The truth is, I didn't want to think about it because I didn't want to be disappointed again. Time and again he would tell me that we would finally get going and the kids could have a real tutor and we wouldn't have to work so hard just to get by. Deep down inside I secretly held the hope that someday if he made it big, he would return me to my mom. So it was easier for me to just concentrate on the jobs I had to do and not ask too many questions. I learned not to ask too many questions to protect myself from constantly being disappointed with his answers that were always vague and repetitious.

The next day, the 25th, I was in the "backyard office" finishing up a print job that was due the next day. The girls were outside playing. Nancy was in the house taking care of Pat, and Phillip was probably also in the house, either sleeping or reading the Bible. It was approximately five p.m. All of a sudden, Nancy came running in to tell me Phillip had been arrested. I was in shock. At first I thought she was joking, but then I saw the worry on her face. I told her to calm down, everything would be fine. Phillip always said if anything ever happened that we just needed to get a lawyer, so I told her we should look in the Yellow Pages for a lawyer and a bail bondsman. I told her that Phillip would use his one phone call to call us and he would tell us what to do. I didn't want to alarm the girls and scare them. I had plenty of practice keeping calm and unaffected on the outside when on the inside I felt anything but calm.

Nancy and I told the girls and they were scared. They had no idea why he had been arrested. None of us did at that point. Throughout the years, the girls and I grew up knowing Phillip was on parole for hurting a woman, was sent to prison for many years, and that the parole agents that came to the house were there to supervise him. And that it was our job to keep the fact that we lived there a secret from the parole agents. So they knew that much. I had been hearing all about his prison experience for years from Phillip.

A few hours later, as we were all sitting in the house trying to be calm and just wait for his call, in walks Phillip and his parole agent through the back porch door. We were stunned and relieved. Phillip was always the one with all the answers and we didn't know what to do without him. Nancy ran to Phillip and put her arms around him while shedding tears of stress and relief; the girls and I watched from the living room as his parole agent uncuffs him, instructs him to report the next morning to the Concord parole office, and leaves. After many hours of holding it together, I finally lost it and started to cry. It probably looked to everyone like I was relieved to have him back, but the truth is on the inside I felt like they were tears of anger. Yes, I was angry! Angry at everything. Angry at the parole agent for taking him and then not taking him. Angry at Phillip for not doing anything to prevent all of this. We relied on him, and I guess in that instant it became clear how much we relied on him and it didn't really look like he cared. It was all about the angels this and the angels that. What about us? It was always the same old thing with him.

On some level I wonder how he possibly could have come back. Perhaps it was true no one remembered me. I know it only fed Phillip's delusions that he was somehow above the law. Phillip believed that all the coincidences surrounding him from his kidnapping of me and getting away with it to present-day things like his parole officers' inability to hold him for anything were not just mere coincidence, but the work of the angels. His theory was that before he took me, he was developing the ability to hear the angels and that in order to shut him up they allowed him to get away with taking me and thus keep him occupied and out of their realm. He thought there was no other way he would have possibly gotten away with his kidnapping that day save for them. I had always believed in the good of angels and this only further confused me. Was Phillip truly special and in the eyes of God worthy of protecting? Or merely making this whole story up to give himself an excuse? What about me? Wasn't I worth anything, or was I merely an object to use?

For the most part, we were all relieved and went to bed thinking it was over. The next morning as I was still sleeping in my tent, Phillip comes out and tells me through the tent window that I need to get dressed because we are all going down to the parole office this morning. He said he was tired of this harassment from the authorities and wanted them to see that everything was okay so he could continue with his "project/mission." I was scared. I didn't know what to say. I got dressed and came inside to find the girls dressed and ready, too. Before we left the property, Phillip had me type up a letter for a lawyer that was based in Concord. He wanted to leave it with him on our way to the parole office, letting him know that his project was moving forward. He added that he would need this particular lawyer's services shortly. Pat was still asleep, so Phillip thought she would be okay until we got back. I asked him what I should say when we get to the parole office. He said to say that I'm the girls' mother and that I gave him permission to have them with him and that, yes, I was aware that he was a sex offender. If asked anything else, he said I should ask for a lawyer and say no more. We all got in the car and he could see I was nervous. He said everything would be fine and we'd get some breakfast on the way home. I couldn't say anything; I just shrugged my shoulders. On the inside I was wondering what he thought he was doing; did he really think we could just walk into his parole office and nothing would happen? But after years of being conditioned to listen to him on everything, it was easy to not say anything. Nancy didn't say anything the whole way up. The girls said everything would be okay. I was nervous that I would say the wrong thing and mess up whatever he had planned. All he kept telling me was to not be afraid and if I was harassed to ask for a lawyer right away. Phillip always planned everything before he did it, so I assumed that he had thought this one out, too.

When we arrived at the Concord parole office we all got out of the car. Phillip marched us in the door of the parole office. I recognized Phillip's parole officer coming toward us. Confusion registered on his face when he saw that Phillip had brought minors into the office with him. He asked me, the girls, and Nancy to please come with him to the back. He said children were not permitted in the waiting room. As we were being led away from

Phillip, I remember looking back at him and asking with my eyes what to do. He winked at me. That was all. The parole agent led us into a private room and asked what we were doing here. I told him all the things that Phillip told me to say. I gave him the name Allissa because that was the name I had been using since G was born. It was the name that our clients knew me by. After he questioned mostly me for about twenty minutes, asking questions like who I was and what was my purpose for staying with the Garridos, he decided to let us go and gave me his card and told us we could leave.

We went out the back way and sat in the car willing Phillip to walk out of the building so we could return home. I still could not fathom what the outcome of that day would turn out to be. Nancy was strangely quiet, and I asked her if I did okay with talking with the agent. She said I did really good and she couldn't think of anything I could have added. She didn't understand why Phillip had brought us all in the first place. Phillip never walked down those steps.

Instead, two parole agents came out. One was the one that questioned me, and he had a partner with him. When we saw them coming, I asked Nancy what she thought I should say or do. She said I could pretend to be a distant relative of Phillip's mother from Missouri. When the two agents arrived at the car, they asked us to get out of the car. I looked at Nancy and asked her what we should do. She said she didn't know. While the new agent asked the girls and Nancy to sit on the curb, Phillip's parole officer asked me to step away with him because he had a few questions for me. I felt like I was in big trouble. He said that I had been lying to him. He said that I was not the mother of these kids. I looked him in the eye and stated, "I gave birth to both of those girls and that makes me their mother!" He said Phillip said that all three of us were actually his brother's kids. I didn't know what to say. I couldn't think of a reason why Phillip would say such a thing after he had told me to tell everyone that I was the mother of the girls. I felt like he abandoned me.

I started to think that I was in real danger of getting separated from my girls because this man did not believe me. He thought me a liar. I thought this man would take the kids from me if he thought I wasn't their mother, so I started to fight. And that's what I tried to do even though I hated to tell this man lies, I did my best to convince him. I am not proud of that today, but I did what I had always done . . . tried to survive an impossible situation. I told him that Phillip was lying for me, that I was running from an abusive husband, and I didn't want anyone to know where I was. I went on and on. By this time, the kids were really scared. My youngest daughter had to go to the bathroom. The officer said to walk with him to the bathroom. We started walking, and I tried again to convince the officer to let us go. He said he had to call CPS [Child Protective Services]. Phillip spent years trying to convince me he was the one with all the power and answers. I was so scared, and even though I was so close to having my life back, I still could not crash through the wall that he built inside of me.

A new female officer came, and the kids and Nancy were separated from me. In some strange way, it felt like I had become the suspect. I was alone in a room all by myself. I thought I would never see my kids again. The officer thought I had taken the kids and run away from somewhere. The officers said that if

I didn't tell them my name and the truth, I would be taken down to the police station and fingerprinted and then they would find out who I was. I didn't know what to do. I asked to see Phillip. They brought him in handcuffs into the room I was in. I looked at him. I asked him in front of the officers what I should do. I told him they might take the girls away from me and I couldn't let that happen. I didn't know what to do. He had always been the one with all the answers. Now all he did was look at me with dead eyes and said I needed to get a lawyer. They took him away. After what seemed like another hour of me sitting in a room by myself, apparently giving me time to think about my situation, they sent a woman officer to come talk to me.

During that time alone I was beginning to realize that Phillip was gone and that I was on my own and needed to take care of my girls. But I had been so conditioned to protect Phillip and Nancy that telling a stranger my story was not easy for me and I could not do it at first. I had asked for a lawyer several times, but the answer I kept getting was, Why did I think I needed a lawyer if I said I didn't do anything wrong?

The woman officer was sympathetic and reassured me that my kids were okay and that I would see them again. I told her I didn't know what to do. She asked again for my name and I told her I couldn't tell her. She told me everything happens for a reason and that everything was going to be okay. She left. I was alone again. She came back a while later. It felt like an eternity. I must have gone to the bathroom a million times. When she returns she tells me Phillip has confessed. She said, "He confessed to kidnapping you several years ago." She asked me again for my name and asked how old I was when I was kidnapped. I felt like

I had just been waiting for the right question, and I said I was eleven and that I was twenty-nine now. She was shocked. She asked for my name again. I said I couldn't say it. I wasn't trying to be difficult. I told her I haven't said it in eighteen years. I told her I would write it down. And that's what I did. Writing shakily on that small paper, the letters of my name:

JAYCEE LEE DUGARD

It was like breaking an evil spell. In that moment, I felt free but also exhausted and completely alive all at the same time. Talk about an emotional roller coaster. I wrote down my name for the first time in eighteen years. She also had me write down my date of birth and mother's name. I looked at her and said, I can see my mom? She said, Yes!

After they had my name and realized who I was, they quickly reunited me with my girls. I was so relieved. Plans were made to take me and the girls over to the Concord police station where everyone thought we'd be more comfortable.

At the police station, I was given a room to wait in while the girls were entertained in the front office. I guess they felt like I needed some time by myself. During this time, I was visited by many people including the female officer that I had given my name to. I didn't know why I was waiting in that room. I was asked for my story a few times, and I recounted as much as I could in all instances. During one of these visits I met Officers Todd and Beth. They came to introduce themselves and asked if there was anything I needed. At first I said no but then I re-considered because I could hear G in the other room talking to anyone that would listen about how worried she was about her hermit crabs back at the house. I asked Officer Todd if it was possible to get the hermit crabs from the house and let her have them, and he said he would see what he could do. I was also very concerned about our cats and the two dogs I had been taking care of for J, the neighbor. The two officers said they would try to get some answers for me. Alone again the tears I had been hold-ing back finally came pouring out, no longer waiting for permis-sion to fall.

Next step involved me, a phone, and two officers from the El Dorado County Sheriff's office. It was the much-anticipated phone call to my mom. I was really running on adrenaline by then; I couldn't eat the food that was offered, I think I had taken a sip of a Dr Pepper. My stomach was tied up in knots. The of-ficers first asked if I had any questions about anything and the question that popped into my mind and I asked was, "Is my mom still with my stepfather, Carl?" I was informed that my mom and Carl had been separated for years and no longer lived together. I was relieved because I had been anxious about going back to a house with Carl there. I had come to resent him for always trying to separate me and my mom when I still had time with her.

In the room with the two officers and the phone sitting on the desk, all I could think of was "Mom." That one word was swimming round and round in my head. I had so much I wanted to say, but as I sat there listening as the phone rang, it felt like my tongue weighed a thousand pounds. The first call was placed to her house. The phone rang and rang and just when they were prepared to cut the connection and try a different number, the phone picked up and a female voice answered, "Hello?" The officers ask for my mom and it sounds like the voice on the other end says she is at work and can be reached there. The officers ask if this is her daughter and when they get the answer "yes," they proceed to tell her the reason for calling. I am sitting there listening, thinking that I cannot believe they are talking to my baby sister. There were times in the backyard that the people I loved took on an almost dreamlike state and became not real but imaginary people from my past. The officers concluded the call by saying that they would be in touch again as soon as they got ahold of our mom and hung up the phone. The next call they placed was to my mom's workplace in an attempt to contact her. This time they were put through to her and by the time I heard her voice on the other line, I was at a complete loss for words. I don't even remember what I said. I've asked my mom since and she told me that I said I had babies. I can't believe I said that! I meant something completely different, not that my kids were babies, but I just wanted her to know I wasn't alone and that I came with kids and in a way that was my attempt to see if she would accept them with me. I knew I would never leave my kids and if my mom rejected them for some reason, I didn't know what I would do. I wanted her desperately, but I was also a mother with a responsibility to my girls. Luckily, that turned out to not even be an issue and we were all accepted with open arms. I believe I also got out the words, "Come quick!" I remember hearing her screaming on the other end that "My daughter has been found!" over and over and then I said "I love you!" and that's all I remember from the initial call to my mom. I wish I could remember every moment, but my mind was on overload.

Officer Todd arranged for the three of us to stay at a hotel that night, and as we left the CPD, we drove past a news van and barely missed being discovered. When we arrived at the hotel, Todd's partner, Beth, who we had also met at the CPD, brought us some pajamas and toiletries. Todd pulled me aside and mentioned that the girls weren't eating because I wasn't eating and that if I ate, it would help them. So I announced I was hungry and we decided on enchiladas for dinner. I could only force down a couple of bites, but at least it was something. And the girls ate. We were left alone together for the first time all day, and I was encouraged to tell the girls what was happening and why. I tried to explain everything to them in a way I thought would be right. As we sat on the bed together that night and I recounted to them all that their dad was responsible for, they were surprisingly open to all that I said and didn't really seem surprised to hear any of it. I told them that the days ahead would be tough on them both and me, too, but that I would do all I could to make the right decisions for our future and no matter what, we would be together. I told them I would never leave them.

A knock on the door brought more people to meet, these two being the victim advocates assigned to me and my daughters. After introductions, we were left to our own privacy again.

I was nervous about the reunion the next day with my mom and sister, who I was desperate to meet. The girls were very supportive and excited for me. They slept in one bed together, leaving me to toss and turn in the other bed. I don't think I slept more than a few minutes that night. I had a terrible sinus headache from crying for several hours. Questions like: What if my mom doesn't accept the girls? What if my mom hates me? What if my mom is still with Carl? Could I have tried harder to leave? . . . That night, many thoughts and fears and guilty feelings regarding Phillip and Nancy tried their best to implant themselves in my head, and it left me feeling exhausted by morning. My world had turned upside down, and I didn't know what to do. I had fears for my daughters. Would I be able to protect them in the outside world? I always had Phillip to protect them for me when we went out. And all of a sudden it was just me. Everyone that I had encountered had been so nice and I felt protected with them, but I had a fear it would end soon and I'd be alone.

The next day finally came after a long and restless night. I was so nervous my stomach was full of butterflies. Would I recognize her? Would she remember me? Would she like the person I had become? Would she be mad at me? Would she accept my girls as her grandkids? I had so many questions and thoughts. Too many for my mind to process. When I was told that my sister and my aunt had come with my mom, I was so excited and nervous that I had to remind myself to breathe. Every time someone would say the word "mom" I would burst out crying. The FBI agents that had been brought in said they were going to brief her and then I would be able to see her. The briefing seemed to take forever, but the time finally came. With a last encouraging hug from each of the girls I followed one of the many people to the elevator. Prior to that I was asked if I prefer to meet my mom alone initially, and I said that I would like that and to please bring the girls in later. Once downstairs I was escorted to the door of the room she was in. I'm not sure if I truly believed that my mom was in that room waiting for me. I was convinced that this day would never happen. On the threshold of the room I was frozen for a minute, I couldn't move. I just stared wide-eyed at the door. Finally, I took a deep breath and I made myself walk through the door. And there she was! I knew it was her instantly. For the longest time I couldn't remember what she looked like. I would try to draw her, but her face wouldn't come to mind. Sometimes different aspects of each of my daughters reminded me so much of my mom, but I couldn't pinpoint exactly what it was because I had forgotten what she looked like. But there she stood, with arms wide open. I walked to her and she was smiling and crying and she put her arms around me and I felt so safe and whole again. Even now just writing about it brings tears to my eyes. I told her she smelled the same, she said it was smoke, but it was more than that—I remembered her scent, like I remembered from when I was young. It was the same; she was my mom and she was holding me. The whole experience felt surreal.

As we stood there crying on each other's shoulders, she pulled back a little to look me in the eye and hold on to my shoulders. She said to me, "I knew I would see you again. Do you remember when we used to sit outside on the porch swing and talk about the moon as it rose high in the sky? Well, when you were taken from me, I used the moon to talk to you. I've been talking to you for so long. The other night the moon was full and bright and I asked the moon, Okay, where are you, Jayc? The next day I get the call that you have been found." I look at her astonished. I tell her I remember that moon, too. I was walking out to my tent and for some reason I looked up and stared at the moon for a few minutes. It seemed strange to me at the time because I usually avoided looking at the moon. I tell her that it was too painful because it brought back memories of her. But that moon was so bright it caught my eye. "Now I'm here with you."

We hug some more and then sit down to catch up on our many years apart.

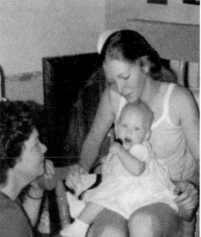

Memories with mom

Firsts for Me

My life has changed so much since last summer. I am free to be a mother to my girls. I am free to drive. I am free to say I have a family. My family is my own. I have my daughters, my mom, my sister, and my aunt. I am rebuilding relationships with my extended family and friends. I have met so many new people. It's amazing to know so many people and to count some of them as my close friends. For so long I was confined to knowing just a few people. When I was in captivity, there were times that I longed to talk to the girl at the cash register if only about the weather, but Nancy was always there with me, and I know it would have gotten back to Phillip. And then the lecture would ensue. I've learned that verbal abuse can be just as damaging as physical abuse and take longer to heal from. But I'm doing that as well. I'm healing from the physical and verbal abuse I endured for so long. It has not been an easy road. I got lucky, though, by being placed with a psychologist who has a unique approach to traditional therapy, and I believe she is a big part of why I am making as much progress as I am. With her help I am learning to speak up for myself—something that if I did before was always met with opposition and Phillip telling me why I was wrong. It's hard to stand up for yourself when all the other person does is tell you how wrong you are and give you reasons why he is right. I'm now able to make decisions for myself and my girls, and although they have not always been the right choices, they were still mine to make and that feels good despite the bad decision. One example of this is going to Sly Park with my daughters for a friend's birthday campout. I wanted to go but was warned about the dangers of the paparazzi and snapping some pictures. I am headstrong and I wanted my girls to be able to see the Perseid meteor shower in the darkness of a campsite, so I chose to take them. We had a fabulous time camping out under the stars. We laid our blankets and sleeping bags and watched as the flashes of light darted across the sky. We also played in the lake and ate pie for dinner and hamburgers for dessert! We had a great time together and didn't realize our privacy was being violated. Upon returning home and learning of the pictures that were taken that weekend, I was immediately saddened and embarrassed. I also felt horribly that I had inadvertently put my girls in the public eye again. What was supposed to be a fun trip before school started turned into a nightmare. Thank goodness for Nancy Seltzer, my public relations manager. She was able to get the girls' faces blurred in the tabloid pictures, saving them from unwanted attention. All I want is for my girls to have the privacy and freedom they deserve in the days ahead and, thanks to NS, we can have that awhile longer.

Another emotion I felt during that ordeal was doubt in myself. I felt I could no longer be trusted to make sound decisions. I felt that because I had made the decision and it turned out to be the wrong choice, then all my future choices would be no good, too. It took a few sessions with my therapist to get me to see that it was okay to make the decision I did. That it was better that I went despite some advice that it could be dangerous because it was a public place, because if I had not gone and heeded the advice I was given, I would never have truly known if it was safe or not to go and would have resented the advice. So it was better to have made the decision I did and learn from it. Also, not all choices are black and white. We all have the right to make up our own minds about stuff, but it's better when you have all the facts and go in to make an informed decision. Looking back, I should have researched where Sly Park was and asked some questions about how public it was before I made the decision to go.

Milestones

Even though I was closed off to the outside world in the backyard, the outside world did find a way to touch us. I remember 9/11, the day the terrorists flew planes into the Twin Towers, killing all those people. I remember exactly where I was when Phillip came running outside to tell me. He yelled in his sad voice, "Allissa, did you hear? Someone just crashed a plane into one of the Twin Towers!" I was outside going to pee in my pee hole. My outdoor toilet was full and Phillip didn't like to empty it very often. I made myself a pee hole outside, so I was out there when I heard the news. I rushed back in the studio and the news was on channel three. They were showing pictures of the buildings smoking and helicopters circling. It was so scary. I kept on thinking, I wonder what else they were going to bomb. And who had done it? Then the news reporter started talking about all the people that were trapped inside and I started crying. Phillip and Nancy were crying, too. Phillip said the "angels" made those terrorists do what they did and that's why he had to expose the "angels" to the world one day. It made more sense than anything else in the world did at the time.

Other than 9/11, there were no real "events" in my life to recall. I didn't really have any of the typical milestones that other kids enjoy. Like first crush, first date, getting my driver's license. I remember, I think I was twenty-one or twenty-two and I had gone with Phillip for the drive to the paper place where we got our paper for the printing business in Concord. We got stuck in traffic coming home. Traffic always makes me feel sick. I felt like I was going to throw up, so he pulled over for a minute. He said it was too bad I was sick because he was going to teach me how to drive that day. I was feeling too sick to say anything, so I just shrugged. On the inside I was so disappointed. I wonder if he really was going to teach me to drive that day. I always wanted to learn how to drive. My girls always thought it was weird that I didn't know how to drive yet. They would ask me why, and I would say because I didn't want to and maybe one day I would. What else could I say? They asked their dad, too, but he would say something like, "Allissa will be able to learn how to drive one day and I am really looking forward to that day." Again I would wonder when that day would ever come. One time I was out shopping with Nancy and she said, why don't you sit in the driver's seat and give it a try? I was a little scared. I was probably twenty-five or twenty-six at the time and had never even sat in the driver's seat before. It was a foreign concept to me even though I longed to be able to drive. I did get in the driver's seat and she said to start it up, and I did, but I guess I hit the accelerator a little too hard and almost backed into the truck that was coming in behind us. Nancy got a little freaked out and that was the last time she let me try. So I didn't learn to drive until I was twenty-nine and out in the real world.

I can't say I remember turning sixteen. I was already a mom. My oldest daughter was almost two by then. I also never got the chance to graduate from high school (although I do hope to earn my GED one day).

I do remember, however, when my sister, Shayna, turned sixteen. I was twenty-six and by then living in Phillip's secret backyard in my own tent! I loved the freedom of having my own room. When the printing business was making good money, Phillip would give me and Nancy an allowance to spend. I bought roses to put around my tent and used the bamboo growing in the back to make my own fence surrounding my room. I planted morning glories, purple ones, and they grew up to engulf my makeshift fence of bamboo. I made a walking path of stones to the front of my room, so when it rained I wouldn't get sand in there. I had my own things, and Nancy and I would go thrift store shopping for clothes, knickknacks, and shoes.

I remember waking up on January 16th, 2006, and the very first thing I did that morning was say out loud to nobody in particular, 'cause I was all by myself out there, I said, "Happy Sixteenth Birthday, Shayna!" I really wished I could be there to celebrate with her on that day. I wondered what she looked like and if she was happy. I wonder if she had a sweet sixteen birthday party. I so wanted to be with her on that day. That's all I could think about all day for some reason. Phillip Garrido took many things from me, and watching my sister grow up was one of them. I have loved my sister since the day she was born and dreamed about one day being her best friend. I was always a shy kid and she represented a twenty-four-hour companion for me. Although it was hard sometimes to watch how much Carl loved her more than me, that didn't change my feelings toward her. I have never really thought of her as my half sister, she's always just been my little sis. I wanted so much to do things with her. Like, I couldn't wait for her to get older, so we could ride the bus together. I would see the other girls with their sisters and couldn't wait for the day when I could introduce my little sister to them. Or if my sister was being picked on, as her older sister I could come to the rescue and chase away all the bullies. I had so many plans for us, but all of it was stolen away.

When I saw my now grown-up little sister for the first time at age nineteen, I was amazed. She was so beautiful and tall. She was wearing white that day. My first thought: I wonder if she's a nurse? But I learned later she wasn't. She was still in college and trying to decide what she wants to be in this world. I think she should take all the time she needs to figure that out. She's very smart and perceptive. It has been hard getting to know her. I have been so busy with my own kids, and she has a life of her own. From her perspective: She was a baby when Phillip took me from our family. She never knew me. She grew up hearing about her sister "Jaycee" that was kidnapped when she was eleven years old, but she didn't remember me. On the other hand, I remember her and I remember playing with her as a baby. I just didn't know the person she grew up to be. We have plenty of time to

*Me and Shayna,
the year I was
taken*

build a lasting friendship. The base is already there, which is our deep love for one another; the rest will come with time.

Snapshots of a stolen life

My sister Shayna actually taught me to drive. How ironic is that—my little sister teaching me, her big sister by ten years, to drive. It was great, though. She was the first one to say, Come on, let's go for a drive. And she was an awesome teacher. She was very relaxed and calm. I was shaking and scared to death the first time I got into my mom's car (yes, I used my mom's car). I was giddy with joy, and adrenaline was pumping through my veins. I was ecstatic. I learned to drive on a very winding lane. I think in the long run that was great experience for me. After I received my driver's license, thanks to the generosity of a complete stranger, I was given the incredible gift of a brand-new car! To me my car is much more than just a car; to me it represents my newfound *freedom*. I can now take my girls places and go where I want to go anytime.

By the time I got my license, I wasn't the best driver, but I was a very cautious driver. Still am. In fact, my mom teases me about my "two hands on the wheel and looking straight ahead" driving style. But I like to be cautious and careful. Driving is becoming much more comfortable for me now, and I feel like I could drive just about anywhere, which is so cool. I am now driving my kids back and forth to school every day. How amazing is that! Who would have thought I would be actually driving my girls to school and packing their lunches and being able to take a walk with them whenever we want. It just really amazes me that I am now free.

The Difficult Parts of Life

Do you ever think twice before going to your child's football or basketball game? Do you ever have to think, Am I putting my kids' future in jeopardy because I show up at a game? I have to think about that every time I step out of the house. Am I doing something today with my kids to cause them to get their photo taken and jeopardize their privacy? I know this is not a life-or-death situation, but it is hard for me nonetheless. Now that I can, I want to be there for them in all the ways I couldn't before—watch them play ball and help out with school functions—but I can't without risking someone will recognize me and connect me with them. Sometimes I feel like I'm still a prisoner. Yes, I could decide to say screw it and to hell with what happens. But I really don't have that choice. It is a free country and as such people have the right to take your picture or your kids' picture and sell it for the highest price. I spent eighteen years hiding and not being seen, and now it almost feels like history is repeating itself. I know that sounds dramatic and maybe it is, but it kills me inside to tell my daughters we can't do something together because I can't risk them being connected with me. I know it's not the end of the world. I will get through this. It will be an exercise of saying no, putting my foot down, and saying it's just too risky—something so simple. People watch their children's games, go to a school fair, host a spaghetti feed, and don't even think twice. Some may grumble and rather be in my shoes and some just take it as a normal duty as a parent.

I feel I have missed out on so many things already that I hate to miss a second more. But I have to keep my girls safe and their lives normal. Sometimes I have trouble untangling my past and my present. My past was spent hiding and feeling nervous when I was out in public. I had been conditioned to blend in and not draw attention—change my hair color, wear a wig, put on glasses, and wear a hat. Now it is mostly the same. Inside, I fight a war about being the person I want to be and tempering that with who I need to be to keep my kids safe. When will the battle end?

Finding Old Friends

Officer Todd and a friend were able to sneak my youngest daughter's hermit crabs into the hotel room while we were there. Todd contacted a fellow officer that was assigned to the search of the property and told them where to find them. That officer found the hermit crabs and brought the tank back to the station. The next day Todd and his friend smuggled them into the Hilton. They walked it past the front desk using a luggage carrier with towels covering the ten-gallon tank, then up in the elevator they went. When they knocked on the door, the room was already filled with people, from FBI, to police, to victim advocates. The room barely had standing room. People had to make way as Todd and his friend rolled the precious cargo inside the room. G was sitting on the bed and as Todd lifted the towel off the tank, the biggest smile I had seen in a long time spread across her face. G dubbed Officer Todd "Royal Crab Carrier One" and Todd's friend "Royal Crab Carrier Two" right there on the spot.

Officer Beth was able to keep track of our cats and the neighbor's dogs for us, too. The animal shelter the cats were at spayed and neutered them for us and gave them all their shots. There were six cats rescued from the property all together, four of our new kittens and two adult cats, Patches and Lily, who were strays that I fed. Beth asked what I wanted to do about the two dogs, and since I never really felt they were mine, I asked if she could find good homes for them. Which I later found out she did. Patches turned out to have nose cancer and the animal shelter volunteered treatment for him. I was torn at the prospect of never seeing any of them again, but I also knew I had no home, no money, and I had no idea what our future held. The girls were adamant they wanted to at least keep the kittens. I asked Beth if she could find foster families for our cats until we were more settled and she said, "No problem." We were reunited with our kittens January '10. Beth adopted Patches, who has since survived the nose cancer and who has found his family. Lily was adopted by a friend of Beth's and is living a happy carefree life.

My oldest daughter's parakeet was returned to her and she has had him ever since. Beth also told me the ambulance had come for Phillip's mother and she was being cared for.

After my initial shock at being reunited with my mom, sister, and aunt, I began to wonder what happened to my best friends, Jessie and Shawnee. Jessie had been such a constant of my early years that a part of me never forgot about her and I thought of her often. Shawnee was the last friend I had, and I was curious as to how her life was now. I enlisted the help of my new friend Todd.

A few weeks after our recovery, Todd asked me if there were any friends I would like him to find, and I said I would like to find Jessie and Shawnee. He had no trouble finding Shawnee on Facebook and soon told me that she was married with a couple of kids. He said he had contacted her on Facebook and left a number for her to call. I guess she was a little suspicious of that because she had her lawyer call and check him out first, but when she found out that he was indeed a real officer and was calling on my behalf, she accepted. To keep my privacy, Shawnee began sending letters to Officer Todd in care of the police station and he would get the letters to me. The letters eventually turned into emails that he would forward to me. It was wonderful to reconnect with her and hear that she was happy with her two kids and married to a wonderful guy. I learned that she had lost her grandma Millie, who I remember living with in Tahoe, and she had also lost her mom a few years back. But she made a wonderful life for herself and I am so happy for her. I called her on the phone for the first time on November 5th, 2009. I invited her to my daughter's birthday; she couldn't come down at that time because she also had a couple of birthdays to celebrate, and so we made plans for her to come down and visit in December. When I saw her for the first time, she looked so much the same I would have recognized her anywhere. She had a huge surprise for me and my family. Her work had pooled together and brought us things we desperately needed. Christmas came early for us all. Todd and his family were there, too, and he brought us each a brand-new bike. It was the best Christmas ever, but it wasn't the presents that made it special; it was being able to see my mom smile and happy and seeing that my sister turned into a beautiful woman and knowing my aunt never forgot me. Knowing I had a family was the biggest and best gift of all.

Todd also found my childhood friend Jessie. She was a little more difficult to find, but he eventually did. She wrote me letters and sent me homemade chocolate chip cookies through Todd and then we started to email. I called her for the first time on November 5th, too, after I got done talking with Shawnee. Did I mention how nervous I was to call either one of them? Even though they had been sending me letters and seemed to remember me, I was still nervous to call either one of them. Todd assured me that they both wanted to talk to me, but still, what if I didn't know what to say? I still didn't feel comfortable using a phone without permission. It's taking some time to realize I don't have to ask permission to do the things I want. I was shaking as I dialed each of their numbers. They both turned out to be very easy to talk to. The call to Jessie lasted an hour and a half. She did most of the talking, but I loved to listen to her talk and tell me about her life. I invited her to come up for G's birthday and she started crying and said she would be there.

Jessie drove nine hours to get to us and brought her seven-year-old daughter and her mom, Linda. As she drove up the driveway, she was so excited she barely put the car in park before she jumped out and ran to me and embraced me in the fiercest hug I had ever had. We were both crying and in that moment I felt an old connection reestablish. It's an odd feeling to know that a certain person will always be there for you, no matter what. It's

hard to describe. My friend was the old Jessie and the new combined. She was taller than me, which bugged me because growing up I had always been taller than her. She still had the same
long dark brown hair and she was skinny just like before. She
looked so much like her mom. After we let go of each other, she
introduced me to her daughter and I introduced my two daughters. My mom and sister were there, too, and we were all hugging
each other. Hugging Linda again was a wonderful feeling, too.
Growing up I had spent a lot of time with her. And hugging her
was like going back in time and smelling the salty sea air where
she used to take us and tasting the sand in our sandwiches as we
sat on the warm beach in Southern California. We talked until
the wee hours of the night. It felt so natural and easy. The next
day she helped decorate for G's birthday party. We had invited all
our new friends including Todd and his family and Beth. It was
crab themed because my daughter loves her hermit crabs Kevin,
Devin, and Cheese.

Therapeutic Healing

Initially I assumed that I would be going home with my mom once we were released. I didn't know what to think of this prospect. Honestly, I was doing what I had always done and was just going with the flow. I had absolutely nothing but the clothes I was wearing, my girls, and $500 that Todd gave me from one of his family members. So I had a total of $500 to my name. My initial reaction to this money was disbelief that a perfect stranger would give me so much. My thought was, "Why would a perfect stranger want to help me?" Officer Todd replied, "People just want to help you. There will be many more." Officer Beth got us toiletries and pajamas the first night of our release, which I was very grateful for. I was scared of everything, to say the least. But deep inside something that had been dormant for so long was finally getting the chance to grow and I felt it glowing inside me.

A light that I thought had been extinguished was slowly coming back to life. Every time things seemed overwhelming, I would look at my mom and that happy feeling came back and the warm light inside grew bigger.

I was told there was a reunification specialist located a couple of hours away from the hotel we were staying at who was willing to work with me and my family. I wasn't sure what to say about this offer. Traditional therapy did not appeal to me. The therapy I kept envisioning consisted of me and a small room and someone I didn't know, which was the last thing I wanted. I felt I had worked through what had happened to me and I had always kept my own counsel and thought I was my own best therapist. I didn't want to meet another stranger. In the day and a half, I had met so many new people that I was really overwhelmed.

Ultimately, what convinced me to seek the help of this person was the mention of horses. The impression I got of this person was that of an older lady with a ranch and horses and plenty of room for us to come and get our feet on the ground for a few days. She was one of a few professionals specializing in the field of reunification in abduction cases. I have to confess that part of me wanted to do something for my oldest daughter that Phillip had always promised her he would do and never followed through on, and that was arranging horseback riding lessons. I figured if this person had horses, then chances are I could probably arrange some lessons. I have loved horses since that summer at Lake Tahoe with Shawnee and that summer that we planned to work on the dude ranch together.

I had another reason for wanting to talk to a psychologist, too. That being I wanted to tell her all about Phillip and ask her professional opinion. Everything I had been through with Phillip was so confusing, and I had always wanted a professional's opinion because in my opinion the psychiatrist he was seeing was doing nothing to really help him, and day-by-day he was increasingly paranoid. Even when Phillip told his psychiatrist that he was hearing voices, nothing changed. Therapy did nothing to help him and certainly did nothing to help us who had to live with his continued delusion. So many things confused me about Phillip and the things he would say. I could never believe Phillip was anything but sane and thought about each and every thing he did before he did it; I felt that something about him was just not right. For example, I had always had my doubts about his special "ability" (i.e.: using his black box to let others hear him speaking with his mind). He always made everything sound totally logical and explained himself in all respects, but I still had my doubts. And all his preaching about how the angels control our thoughts and how they use Satan as a tool to control our minds.

I've learned that Phillip has never taken responsibility for his actions, so he invented a way to explain everything away. That being, his "angel theory." Over time this theory evolved into him thinking that since he could hear the angels in his mind, he figured that others should be able to hear his voice in the same manner, too. After that the creation of the black box started. The black box was a black case with a cassette recorder inside that contained recordings of such sounds as football game cheering, random static from the radio, and other various sounds from the television that he would mix down into one cassette tape that he would play and amplify through speakers in the box. He would also use plastic cups from fast-food restaurants and glue them in the box to make the sound different. Then he would hook up the headphones to the box and take it with him to let others hear his "ability." He used to make me sit in front of the air conditioner with headphones and one of those sound amplifiers called Bionic Ears and just sit there and listen to that sound for hours. He called it "tuning in." He would leave me sitting in front of the air conditioner for hours trying to condition me to hear his voice coming out of it when he returned. He said since he could hear his voice and the angels' voices in his head, that by using an outside device like the sound coming out of the air unit or the big overhead lights in warehouses like Costco and Sam's Club emitting a humming buzzing sound, that allowed him to hear the voices coming from those things as well. I didn't know what to make of all he said. On the one hand, I couldn't just come out and say, hey, you're crazy, I don't hear a thing. I had enough sense to know this would not go well for me. So I tried to hear what he wanted me to hear. I really did try. I sat there, and when he came back and sat in front of me and moved his lips to the words "Can you hear me?" I really did try to hear it. I asked him, "If the sound comes from your mind, why do I need to look at your lips?" He said that my mind needed something to visually interpret into words. For some reason, I accepted this explanation and sat there until my legs fell asleep, trying to hear anything remotely like his voice.

One night, I was so tired I thought I did hear something. He had switched from the words "Can you hear me?" to counting "One, two, and three" and I thought I heard the vague sound of him counting. He told me to hold on to the fact that I had heard him because in the days to come, the angels would make me doubt myself. That was the one and only time I heard him, and now I think I was just so tired and I thought if I told him I heard him, that it would end his obsession. So I convinced myself I heard something that wasn't there. It was the same thing with all our Printing for Less clients, too—they heard what they thought they should hear. It was a "shared delusion," I've come to learn. But my hearing him didn't end his obsession. It only seemed to make him more determined for others to hear his "ability." He started to think God had given him this ability to help others, specifically those individuals that also hear voices but do bad things, such as the woman who threw her three children into the bay. He cited this case frequently as why we needed to "get going" and help these people. So that became our focus and I did try to help him with his cause. I typed flyers and sent emails to mind-control victims as well as others he thought would champion his cause. I did all this while maintaining the printing business. When I would question Phillip about why he didn't go to pastors in the area and tell them his new knowledge that he was gaining from the Bible, it always ended with some excuse as to why things had to be done in a certain order and that it wasn't time. Phillip's "mission" continued right up until the day he brought us to his parole office appointment. Then everything changed.

Meeting with Nancy

I wanted to see her for many different reasons, the biggest being closure. Telling her that what she and Phillip did was not okay in any way. Sitting across from her in that little white room for the first time in over a year felt very familiar. I guess the feeling came from knowing her longer than I had known my own mother. But I was nervous and excited and overjoyed and thankful to see my mom for the first time; seeing Nancy did not feel in any way like that. Seeing Nancy felt almost like nothing. I think that I felt like that because there was really nothing solid between us. Our whole time together was a lie—a make-believe world that her husband created to satisfy his needs. Our relationship was built on a house of cards. One good blow and you find the pieces scatter in the wind quite easily. Those are my feelings toward Nancy: there was really nothing solid and there is nothing for me to hold on to now. At first when we were separated at the Concord police station, I was consumed with guilt and my feelings were unsure of themselves. At the meeting she kept calling me Allissa and I would say, "No, my name is Jaycee," and she looked at me and said she was sorry and said it was hard for her to remember, and then she did it again and I corrected her again. I think in total she called me Allissa three times and in each instance I would correct her. She said she knew in her heart that something was going to happen at the parole office that day. I said that it was time, that we couldn't have continued like we were for much longer for the girls' sake. She asked if the girls ever think of or mention her, and at first I didn't know what to say, I looked down and then back up at her, and she said, "They don't, do they?" with these really sad eyes. I looked back down in my lap and told her the truth. I didn't try to sugarcoat it. I said that it's not really an issue right now, but if when they get older and wish to contact her, then that is their choice, but right now it hasn't been an issue. I said what she and Phillip did to me confuses them and they really need her to come clean with anything else she knows about Phillip. I told her Phillip is not the man he portrayed himself to be. He never was. He used his con game for his first victim and then again on Katie Calloway, the victim he was in prison for before he kidnapped me. It's always been about what's best for him. All those times he would say the angels protected him that day that he took me from the hill never once did he even think that I was the one in need of protection that day. I also asked her what was the thing that Phillip would say . . . something about how if I knew about something he did, I would never feel the same about him again . . . She looked at me at first and said, What thing? I repeated my question again and she thought for a minute and then looked up at me and asked if I really wanted to know what that was and I said, Yes I do, I want to know. And she said she had caught him once torturing an animal, and I said was it one of my cats, and she nodded her head a few times in the affirmative and then said, "No, no it was a mouse I caught him torturing," and I said, "A mouse?" She said, "Yes, it was a mouse." I didn't expect that answer. But all I said was, Doesn't that make you wonder what else he did? How about all the times we didn't know where he was? If he could hurt a helpless animal, doesn't that make you wonder what else he was capable of? And she said yes, it did make her wonder. I'd like to believe she felt badly for me all those years, but in a way it was always a selfish act on her part. Yes, she didn't want me to go through all that, but to turn a blind eye to what she knew he was doing to an eleven-year-old girl. How could she entertain little girls in the van and videotape them doing the splits and other things, all for her husband? I guess she just convinced herself that she was doing it for love. To me that is not love. You do not follow someone blindly as they lead you over a cliff. She said that she was scared when I walked in because she thought that I would hate her. I told her although I do not hate her because I do not want to pollute my body with hate, what she and Phillip did to me and my family was unforgivable. That my mom suffered more than any person should have to suffer and my sister and aunt, too, and the other members of my family. She said she hoped one day that my mom could forgive her, and I said I wouldn't hold out for that. She told me that call her crazy, but she still loves Phillip. I told her she needed to stop thinking of what's best for Phillip because he is going to be in jail for the rest of his life and to start thinking about what was best for her, and if she wanted to see her brothers again and have a relationship with her family that Phillip tried to separate her from. I told her to take care of herself. And I told her good-bye for the last time; I told her I would not be back. That although we didn't get to say good-bye to each other at the parole office, that this is good-bye forever. And then I stood up and walked out.

Reflection

So much has happened since that meeting. For the most part I've been able to focus on my daily life, but in the back of my mind I know that I might eventually have to face Nancy again. Walking away that day confirmed my right to make my own decisions. The fate of Phillip and Nancy was truly out of my hands. I realized in that moment how much I have grown when Nancy's attorney felt it necessary to challenge me to call him. The El Dorado County Sheriff's Office supported me to make my own decisions. I know I owe the Garridos nothing and can't understand why Nancy's attorney felt it necessary to ask me to support the very people who abducted me.

Therapeutic Healing with a Twist

The days following our recovery were a time of limbo for all of us. I really didn't want a therapist. I felt I had come to terms with what happened to me and I just didn't want to relive it. Boy, was I wrong. Once I sat down and talked to the therapist they brought in, I realized I did want someone to talk to. I responded to her authentic and down-to-earth personality. Neither she nor her colleague treated me like I was special or damaged in some way. I wasn't the main focus of the group or singled out in an odd way.

Reunification was unique in the fact that it focused on getting my feet on the ground, and during the reunification work we focused on reconnecting me to different facets of my family and dealt with the everyday practical things that I had not been accustomed to such as getting the kids their shots and overall checkups, which we never had the opportunity to do before. The girls had never been to a doctor before. We also went to see a dentist and got our teeth checked out. All of our teeth were in pretty good shape. The only potential problems the girls had were some pits where cavities could possibly develop, but other than that they had good strong teeth. I think one of the main reasons for that is, Phillip instilled the good habit of chewing sugar-free gum from a very early age in them. He was very proud of himself for reading that in a magazine about health and knew that he wasn't going to be taking them to the dentist, so he thought of a way to make it work for himself. My teeth are in pretty good shape, too. I had a lot of dentist chair time when I was little and I still have my original fillings. They have lasted a really long time, and it really surprised me to find that out because I thought fillings only lasted a few years, but these have lasted me more than eighteen! I have never been very fond of the dentist—I can't say it's something I ever missed—but the dentist that they took us to was very nice, and her office was open and not closed in like I remember my old dentist's office being. The girls had no trouble either. So their first trip to the dentist was a success.

I really wanted stability. Not just for the girls but me, too. It took me a while to figure out that the choice to stay in the area that we had been relocated to or go back down south, where my mom, sister, and aunt currently lived, was mine to make. I had never really had that choice before and the concept was new to me. My aunt went back to where she and my mom lived to make preparations for my return. During the time she was away, I made up my mind that I did not want to return to the Los Angeles area. I had come to love the beautiful place in which I was temporarily living. Even with the generous donations we had been receiving in the mail, we still did not have enough money to buy a home or even rent one. National Center for Missing and Exploited Children (NCMEC) stepped in, and a house was found in a secluded part of the town in which I wanted to stay. It was a beautiful old white farmhouse. It was private and there was plenty of room to play or walk outside without the neighbors getting curious, unlike the first house they housed us in when the FBI and El Dorado County first brought us to the area. The only rental they could get was right in the middle of town and not very private. Rentals were hard to come by because it was Labor Day weekend. The house was also full to the brim with FBI and victim advocates. When we moved into the new farmhouse, it was much quieter. Only one FBI agent came with us. We had come to really enjoy her company and now that she has been reassigned, we all miss her very much. She made us feel safe and protected. Living together in the farmhouse, we started to learn how to be a family. We had to get used to each other's different habits and ways of doing things. It took time and work with the reunification team. During that time I was presented with the opportunity to sell a photo to *People* magazine. I was leery at first. I was still unsure about how I felt about anything. The only things that were clear to me were that my mom loved me and the girls and that I really wanted to stay where we were. I wanted to find some permanence. The media was a constant threat. I was told that if I didn't give them a picture, then they would find a way to just take it. I was free yet not free. For the time being, nobody except for the girls and other people with whom we had come into contact knew what I looked like. It felt like I had a ticking time bomb on my head just waiting to go off. I wanted to do things with the girls, but I couldn't. The authorities were worried I would be recognized somehow. I was told I needed a lawyer to be a go-between with the media. They were hounding for a photo and would not give up. After many sleepless nights I decided to sign with *People* magazine. I would give them one photo and a statement.

The day before the shoot, I had second thoughts and decided I did not want to do the photo shoot or give a photo. I was scared. I talked to my lawyer, and he said I could not back out now, that my name would be mud in the media's eyes, and I needed to do the photo shoot. He said that everything would be fine. I said I have not signed a contract, and he said one was being drawn up and I'd have it soon. I realize now that I could have just not shown up. However, in a way, I wanted to be seen finally. I wanted everyone to know how happy I was and grateful for their support. The day of the shoot, everything seemed to go by in a flash. Security was hired and also used to take the photos of my mom, sister, and me together. My therapist has a little dog that goes to work with her frequently. When the security men showed up with my lawyer to do the shoot, they walked into the backyard and Stella promptly walked over to the one with the camera, lifted her leg, and peed on his shoe. I don't even think he noticed. But Rebecca and I did. The sweet little therapy dog had never or has never done that to another person. That should have been the clue to us to pack up and go. We stuck it out, though, and the cameraman did his best to make me and my mom smile. So many things were happening and in reality, I was happy; I just wasn't happy about the way the whole *People* magazine thing was going. At one point we were down in the corral with the two horses, Velcro and Freesia. Freesia, the brown Hanoverian, kept getting in front of me and the cameraman. She kept pushing me back with her body. One shot shows me ducking underneath her just so I can see the cameraman. Then, out of the blue, I was asked if I wanted to take a photo with the girls. I replied that wasn't part of the deal. But then I didn't want rumors to start about how I am trying to hide the girls, so we posed for one together with our backs to the camera. The whole day was strange, and I was glad when it was over. When the magazine came out I was so happy with all the genuine support from everyone and in the end I was glad I did it. After that, I hired a public relations person and tried to stay out of the media's prying eyes. That has not been easy for me because I love being able to do things with the girls and that is not always possible.

The reunification specialist ended up becoming my personal therapist. And my recovery is an ongoing process that we take one day at a time. The day I came to Rebecca's office to meet her horses, I was hooked.

One of the first things she had us do was brush Velcro and Freesia. But it didn't turn out to be that easy because there was a catch; we had to catch them first. Rebecca loaded us up with their halters and sent us into the pen to go halter them. My daughters were naturals and soon had Velcro haltered and were on their way back before I could even catch up to Freesia, who had it in her mind that she didn't particularly feel like being led around by a bunch of humans that day. The faster I went, the faster she went. So I had to change my thinking. I decided to ignore her and pretend I wasn't really interested. Well, that got her attention, and soon enough she was actually walking up to me. I felt a real victory. My tummy made a flip when I felt her nudge my hand. I thought to myself, Now's my chance. I turned to her and scratched her long sleek nose, and with the halter in my other hand, I slowly brought it up to where I thought it was supposed to be. I had never haltered a horse before and being a tad short I found it a bit difficult to say the least. With me on my tiptoes and Freesia just about done with me, I tried and tried but couldn't figure out how to put the halter on correctly. Rebecca came over to me and asked what was going on. At first, I didn't want to give up. I wanted to do it myself and have that sense of accomplishment. I knew my window of opportunity was running out, so I asked myself, Do I give in and ask for help or let the horse get away? I learned that day that I can be a very stubborn person. Freesia had pulled away from me and was on her merry way before I had made up my mind to ask for help. I turned to Rebecca and she, in turn, suggested I ask one of my family members for help. Since my daughters did so well with haltering their horse, I asked if they would help me with Freesia. This time, Freesia was grazing on some grass and was not paying us humans any mind. Even when I walked over with the girls, she didn't seem to mind the interruption. She just calmly stood there and let the girls pull the halter over her and then they handed me the lead rope and off we went together into the arena to begin something that had already begun.

That session ended up being one of many that brought about several revelations about me and how I viewed the world for so many years. During my time of captivity I couldn't imagine a day I wouldn't be there in that place, doing the same things over and over again. I never thought about asking for help. I wonder why that is? It's hard for me to understand myself.

One particularly eye-opening session was when I created an obstacle in the arena, which happened to be a box made of logs, and the goal was to get the horse in the obstacle using no hands or words. At first Velcro would not go into the box, and I felt this was a metaphor for how I was feeling, not wanting to return to my box/backyard. After about an hour of trying just because I had a task to accomplish and I didn't want to quit, I finally decided that I really didn't want the horse in the box after all and announced I was satisfied with the results of the exercise. We went back to the office and processed what the exercise felt like for me. Later when it was time to leave, it was quite a surprise to see Velcro—that horse that would not go into the box—happily sunning herself right in the middle of it! Earlier as we processed the horse exercise, I did mention to Rebecca how much easier everything seemed and less complicated in the "backyard." I was feeling a lot of pressure to make decisions, and I just wasn't used to the complications of life. Even though I didn't want my old situation back, the reality was the "backyard" was less complicated for me in many ways. And I needed to learn to step out gradually.

In another therapy session, Rebecca brought in a big horse ball and told me that we're having a day of play. I couldn't remember the last time I played just for pleasure. In fact, I couldn't remember a day I did something just for myself. Up until recently life was about making Phillip and Nancy happy and making sure the girls had everything they needed. Rebecca told me to take the ball and just play with the horses, so with the big purple ball clutched in my outstretched hands, I entered the arena and tried to get one of the horses to play with me. I spent a good hour standing in front of Velcro, the docile black-and-white paint, slowly rolling the ball to find that all she did was stand there and look bored. The ball would bounce off her legs and return to me but the "play" was mostly one-sided. During that time, some of my rolls to Velcro would miss her legs and go sailing past her. During one of those times, Rebecca's dog, Skye, would come barreling into the arena and run to the ball that I was running after, and she stopped it and started rolling it back to me. I thought this was more fun than rolling it to a horse that clearly was having none of my antics. So I started playing with Skye, the black Labrador. She was a great ballplayer and we soon had a real game of me throwing the ball up to her and her using her nose to send it flying back to me. During this time Freesia, the beautiful brown Hanoverian, started to become intrigued with the concept of Skye playing with the big round thing and started very slowly to drift our way. Nonchalantly at first, and then later going up to the ball herself when it would get away from either me or Skye. By the end, Freesia was actually nudging the ball herself to return it to Skye. It was an amazing sight to see the dog and horse playing ball together. But I realized something, too: at first I was uncomfortable doing something just for me, and Freesia translated that and was very standoffish, but then as I got more and more out of myself and in the moment, I began to see how important it was for me to take moments just for myself and enjoy the simple pleasures of simply playing.

One horse exercise involving my family was early in the reunification process. It was a time of great confusion and just plain not knowing what was really going to happen to us. The paparazzi were a constant threat, and I had no idea how to handle any of it. Rebecca came up with this exercise to give us a real glimpse of what we were up against. My daughters wanted to stop hiding and just live a normal life. They had had enough of hiding and just didn't understand how relentless the media could be.

The horse exercise started out with all of us receiving buckets. Rebecca warned us that the horses are used to the buckets containing grain, so to be careful because once the horses see the buckets they are going to go after them even if there isn't any grain. In this way, they were like the media. Once the media sees you have information or a story, they come after you even if you don't want to share or even if you really don't have any grain/info. So we all go into the arena with our bright yellow buckets. My sister and my mom went in first, followed by the girls and then me. I was very reluctant because Rebecca pulled me aside and said she was going to fill my bucket with grain. I didn't want the grain/story. I wanted to pass it to somebody else. But who? I couldn't pawn it off on my family. So I entered the arena with the bucket filled with grain/info. At first I tried hiding behind my sister with my bucket and it worked. I was left alone. The horses were busy sniffing in all the other buckets, they didn't notice me. I thought this very appropriate because I don't get noticed anyway. Then my sister stepped aside because the horses were really starting to crowd us and I was spotted and the frenzy began. They knew I was the one with the story/grain. They came at me like they had never seen grain before, and in that moment everyone got to see the sheer force the media could be and we knew we needed to find some help. Rebecca suggested I share and spread the grain/info out among my other family members and then try to keep it away from the horses as long as possible. To me the metaphor was, how long can you keep your info to yourself before the *National Enquirer* comes around and wants it at all costs? It was hard to keep it away from them. I am something they want very badly. My daughter felt like she could handle the media, and Rebecca told her to come with her. They walked a little ways away from the group and she whispered something in her ear; later I found out she was preparing her and telling her what she had planned and how to do it safely. She put more grain in G's bucket and told her to run away with the info/grain. Well, she did and those horses went thundering after her. It happened too quickly for me to panic, but I had a firsthand glance of just how dangerous running away with the story can be. Later we went back to the office to discuss what had happened and how we could better deal with the situation. Contact was made with public relations representative and manager Nancy Seltzer and, thanks to her, we have much better dealings with the media.

Another component to the Reunification process is food. Food can be a real comfort, and I must admit I have used it as a crutch many times in the past. Mint Chocolate is one of my favorite treats. Rebecca's team includes a professional chef, Charles. In one of the tabloid magazines they speculated on what I fed the girls for dinner. TV dinners became their guess. Boy, did they get it wrong. We, in fact, were enjoying some delicious and nutritious meals. I feel it is super important to sit down as a family every night and have dinner together. This is not something we got to do before in the "backyard." Now I feel it is doubly important to instill family dinnertime in the girls while they are still living at home. Hopefully, one day they will pass this new tradition of ours to their own families.

Besides Chef Charles, my mom is an excellent cook as well and makes most of our meals at home.

One of my favorite dishes my mom and grandma used to make me when I was little was tomato dumplings. Now that I am home she is able to make them for me once again. It's a very simple recipe, but one that brings back such happy memories for me.

Tomato Dumplings

1 large can (32 oz.) tomatoes
1 small can (16 oz.) diced tomatoes
2 or 3 cans of biscuits

Heat the big can and the smaller can of tomato juice (you have to cut up the tomatoes in the large can into pieces) and bring to a boil. Pinch the raw biscuits into thirds and drop them into the boiling tomatoes and cook until the biscuits puff up . . . maybe 5 minutes or so. That's it!! So easy, but oh so delicious. I'm hoping my mom will write a cookbook to pass the recipes along.

My favorite thing to do in the kitchen is bake. My aunt has taught me the secret of making scrumptious chocolate chip cookies. It's basically the recipe on the back of chocolate chips with a few tweaks, such as adding a pinch of nutmeg and cinnamon to the dry ingredients. The real secret is to mix them by hand and not with a mixer. Also don't over-mix. The cookies end up coming out of the oven softer.

The first days reunited with my family were a blur. I do remember distinctly encountering some strange food in the refrigerator. In particular, some awful peanut butter in the refrigerator and it didn't occur to me to ask where it came from. Later I found it had been stocked by the Transitioning Families chef. The chef told me later how difficult it had been to stock a kitchen with food that would be comforting to a family he didn't know. We had lived primarily on fast food, which was a challenge for my vegetarian child. The healthy food we ate was inconsistently provided.

During the reunification process the chef began to provide us with a new definition of comfort food. In particular I remember a satisfying morsel of chocolate filled with lemon. In the past comfort food meant half a chocolate cake and the agony that followed. Each day when we went to reunification therapy, we were greeted with fresh scones, cucumber water, and incredible indescribable oatmeal. We began to suspect we were being nurtured through this healthy food.

Often after some stressful therapy sessions, we would all sit down to a delicious home-cooked meal. This time allowed us the space to connect together and the opportunity to regroup. Throughout the process, eating meals together was when we really began to feel like a family. The food often gave us something neutral to talk about. Vegetables we had never heard of were presented with regularity. Foods like fennel, Jerusalem artichokes, golden polenta, and Comté cheese became not only new words in our vocabulary but staples in our diet. The food distracted and entertained us, allowing us to leave ourselves for a bit. Later I heard that the food receipts were being commented on from

Eldorado to Washington, DC. They all wanted to know what was for lunch.

During some of the sessions, Chef Charles would take the kids into the kitchen for baking and prepping for lunch. The kids were finding it difficult to figure out where they fit in as my mom, sister, and I were reconnecting. That step needed to occur before we could really figure out how we all fit in together. The kids relished having a place where they could be useful and learn something at the same time. The kids and I had already spent a good deal of time in family equine therapy, and I felt it was only right they had a break. Chef Charles recently mentioned that on one particular day the girls helped him take down an old corral fence. He innocently mentioned how much they enjoyed that activity. I can't help but wonder about the symbolism of taking down a fence for them. It is refreshing that the chef never speculated.

My growth has not been an overnight phenomenon. Nonetheless, it has slowly but surely come about. In the beginning, everything I had been led to believe from Phillip was about protecting him and his plans. I thought he loved me and the girls. I have come to see his love as not real and only based in his reality when it suited him to love us. But love is not part-time and it's not conditional. I learned this from Mom.

Phillip is narcissistic and only does things that benefit him, and I've come to realize this has been the case all along. I learned when I could and couldn't push. For every argument we had— whether it be about the angels or God, or Nancy or the girls, whatever it might be—I was always the one to give up and hand in the towel. I remember one time I was working on pruning my roses around my tent, and he comes to the back to announce that one of our Printing for Less clients was going to set him up with an attorney to get parole off his back. This was not the first time he said something and then nothing happened, so my reaction was less than what he felt like it should be and he asked why I wasn't jumping up and down. Wasn't I happy that finally we could get going? Well, yes, I would have been if I thought he was really going to follow through, but this was in 2006, and up until then he had several ideas and not one he followed through on. So inside I was not impressed with his declaration. He became very angry and said that there was nothing he could do for me if I wasn't going to be happy. The rest of the day was awful. He moped around mostly sleeping. He told the girls, "Allissa was responsible for my mood, she was letting the angels control her"—that's all part of the way I was manipulated. If I didn't do something right, it was my entire fault for how the rest of the day went. I didn't let those days happen very often, at least not on purpose, but I never really knew what could set him off. Sometimes he would shut the business down for days and wouldn't let me touch the printers or get any jobs done. Even when it would look like I had won a battle, he would act disappointed in me or just shut down for days. It taught me that most days were not worth fighting over. Some of the topics of "discussion" were centered around his belief that the angels existed and controlled our minds. Every bad thing that humans do is due to the angels infecting our minds. When I would ask for him to clarify, it would turn into a long speech about how the angels are men and that they live under the earth and one day he would work with the governments to uncover them. He said they gave him terrible dreams of men raping him in prison and him driving off cliffs. I thought maybe that was his conscience speaking. I always felt with him that there was no other answer but his. He would say we could ask him anything. But can you really ask anything to someone who believes that they have an answer for everything and that that answer is the right one? When it came to the Bible, he would say there is not just one answer but that he could take one answer and make it into something entirely new. Sometimes I know my daughters don't understand why I didn't stand up for myself. It frustrates them, I know. That is something that I am working on in therapy. My assertiveness. Sometimes I feel if I disagree with someone, then I need to have a good reason for doing so and I need to have reasons to back me up. I learned in therapy the word "No" is a complete sentence. I love that! I never thought of that before. I'm the type of person that when something new comes up, I like to think it through and, yes, sometimes I hope the problem will just disappear or solve itself. But given enough time, I will work up the courage inside to deal with whatever new needs attention. I can come up with a solution that works for me and usually works for everyone. It's hard to know what will be a mistake and what will not. With Phillip it was easier to know because I had learned his moods throughout the many years of knowing him. I learned to avoid certain situations that I knew would cause a problem. I notice now that I have to deal with things on my own that I avoid making certain decisions or find the easy way out. In some ways I learned to rely on Phillip and Nancy for so many things that now that it is time to do things for myself, I find it not so easy. In my therapy the horses gave me another example. Sometimes it is my job to catch and halter a horse. This particular horse is sometimes mean and nasty. She's the dominant female of the herd for sure and she knows it, so when she senses that I am not a dominant female, her instinct is to challenge or more likely not give a flying leap what I want. So on my first try, I walk out into her stall, and she immediately rushes away from me. I have the idea maybe if she doesn't see the halter, I will have better luck. I put the halter behind my back and she actually lets me approach her. Her ears are flat down and she moves her head like to say I'm going to bite you! My goal is to learn to control my fears and not show any fear. In a contradictory way I'm afraid, but then again I'm not afraid. I confuse myself sometimes. I know this horse and I know she is bluffing. At least I hope so. I try to put the halter on, but she just puts her butt to me and walks away. I have used grain before, so I go get some grain. That does the trick; she comes walking to me for the grain at which time I slip the lead rope around her neck and wait until she finishes the grain to put the halter on. I slip on the halter and at first don't understand why I can't get the clip on. I think I must have gotten the wrong halter, but I don't want to get the other one because now I have her I can't let go or I will have to catch her again. I yell for some help. Something I wouldn't have done before. Luckily, Rebecca is nearby and brings me another halter. I slip the new lead rope around her neck and drop the other in the feeder. I get the halter on and go to buckle it only to find this one does not fit either. Darn! This must not be the right one either. But I think that couldn't be right because Rebecca gave me the halter and surely she knows which one to use. After several tries of unsuccessfully trying to get the buckle on, I ask a stable boy for help. He is at first confused, too, and takes the halter off to inspect it, exactly what I should have done. He discovers that it is inside out. He right-side-ins it and slips it back on and does the buckle up. Rebecca asks what made me think I couldn't have figured it out myself. It got me to think what I would have done if there was nobody there to ask. Would I have figured that out for myself? I'm so used to having someone do it for me that I don't know the answer to that. All I can do is do better next time. Going out by myself is getting easier. I still prefer company but have learned that when forced to do something or go somewhere by myself, I do fine and feel good about myself for going.

Part of my therapy includes learning as much about Phillip and Nancy and the control they had over me as I can stand. This helps me to come to terms about how confusing life was in the backyard. The more knowledge I gain, the more like an adult I feel. I never got the chance to become an adult. Thanks to Phillip, I missed out on some parts of normal human development and I feel I am making up for lost time. Experiencing things for the first time, like going out shopping by myself. Or even just filling up a tank of gas alone was intimidating at first. I was so afraid I would do something wrong and then get into trouble. But since I'm not in Phillip's environment anymore I have the confidence to tell myself, it's okay to make a mistake or, yes, you can do this. I even find myself not realizing that I can even do a certain thing, like go to a concert with a friend or walk into a place by myself; sometimes I still feel like I have to have someone with me. Those feelings are slowly fading now and I'm doing more and more for myself.

One of my favorite things about therapy is the long walks that I go on with Rebecca. I find myself talking more in those two-hour hikes than ever I would in an office. I'm not sure why this is. One theory I have is that I was cooped up for so many years that I relish the thought of walking for long periods of time and just being outside. I love being outside, whether it's for a run or just sitting and watching my cats play, it's where I prefer to be. My least favorite thing to do is sit in the office and talk, but my therapist has found a way to make it interesting for me. I love metaphors and she has come up with the idea of lighting candles to symbolize my past, present, and future. My past and present were the two candles we started with; she would ask me what I would like to start with or deal with today. I would light up either my past or present depending on my answer. During the last few sessions we've used the candles I've noticed my past melting more and more and becoming duller and duller in light. To me, a lover of imagery, this is my past slowly extinguishing itself becoming something that's been melted. Shifting and changing into something completely different than the way I saw it when it was first lit. Remarkably, my present candle has stayed pretty much exactly the way it was when we first lighted it, which to me, symbolizes continuity. My future candle is a special one. Rebecca gave it to me for my thirtieth birthday. It is the face of a horse and her baby. From the first time I lit it to this day, it has burned brighter than the other two put together. I haven't really thought about what that means entirely other than the obvious; that my future is bright and can contain anything I can possibly imagine.

When I imagine that future, I see myself helping families heal after traumatic situations. Families are like snowflakes:

they come in many shapes and sizes and no two are the same. And like a snowflake, they are very delicate and must be protected and guarded from elements that threaten to destroy their precarious balance. When two or more snowflakes merge, they strengthen their chances of surviving in an ever-changing world. Unlike snowflakes, given the right tools, families can survive through the worst conditions.

What Phillip and Nancy forced us to pretend in the backyard was not a family. Yet by some remarkable fortune, the girls and I do have a bond that kept us together despite our challenging situation. Now that bond is free to grow in an environment of better conditions.

Sometimes I look at my life and what I have and think I don't deserve it. Look at all I have when there are so many struggling just to get by and feed their families. The JAYC Foundation evolved from a deep need to give back all that I was given. A pinecone was my last grip on freedom, so to me they represent what was stolen away from me. Now that I am free, they symbolize life and freedom. They are the seeds of new life and that is exactly what I have: "new life." The pinecone is my reminder that life can always be restarted. But I know I can't heal the world. To me the best place to at least start the healing process is within our own families. Given the right tools, even a family that has been torn apart by unimaginable circumstances can learn to build a new path together. The J A Y C Foundation will be set up to support families willing to come together in a variety of situations and diverse circumstances. My hope is to provide counseling and housing for families and victims of abductions and exploitations during the crucial early days of reconnection. I will work to provide the same type of safe environment my family and I experienced during the early days. It was the simple, real approach that helped us heal and return to each other. Transitioning Families worked with my family in the crucial beginning months reuniting us after eighteen very long years apart. My goal is to help one family at a time, providing the tools and time they need to thrive. Animal rescue has always been a dream of mine. And I find it ironic that I landed in a place that embodies so many of my dreams. I'm hoping to rescue many needy families and animals in the years to come. I hope to encourage others to reach out and help other families and animals, too. It's the simple things that count.

Just Ask Yourself to Care (JAYC).

Acknowledgments

There are so many people I want to thank. First and foremost, I want to thank my mom. Mom, you are the bravest person I know and the ultimate survivor. If I was ever to harbor any hate in my heart, it would be for all that you have suffered because of Phillip and Nancy Garrido. Mom, you never gave up hope that I would one day come home and here I am, so glad to be back. You are everything I remember and more. You have embraced your grandchildren in a way I never believed possible. They truly have a grandmother that loves them unconditionally. I can't thank you enough for all the love and acceptance you have given us. Thank you for supporting me in all the decisions I have made. As a single mother you have always been my hero. I knew in my heart when I stared at the moon that you were still holding on to hope. That hope somehow helped me get by.

I encourage those of you that have had a son or daughter kidnapped to hold on to your hope for as long as you can. NCMEC (National Center for Missing and Exploited Children) was there in the background, helping my mom hold on to her hope. Since my return, this organization has been invaluable to me and my family and many others throughout the years. I thank them from the bottom of my heart.

To my sister Shayna: what can I say? I have missed so many years with you and am now aware of all that you must have sacrificed. While I was captive in the backyard, you were there caring for our mom. You grew up watching our mom shed tears for a sister you hardly remembered, that must have been so confusing. We should have been growing up together; instead we lost the innocence of our childhoods. I don't want to give one more moment to the Garridos. It's time to look toward the future and celebrate happy moments to come. I know when I returned, your life was turned upside down again. Thank you for all the love you gave us during that transition. When you taught me to drive, you gave me the first real sense of freedom I had in eighteen years. Thank you, Sis. I love you.

To my aunt Tina: you are a pillar of strength. When I returned, you were still the grounded loving aunt I remember. It did not surprise me at all that you had supported my mom and sister while I was missing. You were so wonderful when I returned; sitting with you as Mom braided my hair I was reminded of my childhood. The missing years were behind me and I remembered all the wonderful things we did together. Now watching you being an aunt to my children brings happy tears to my eyes. I love you and thank you for being the wonderful person you are.

To my extended family: thank you for giving me the space and consideration to relearn who I am. You have all allowed me the time I needed to explore this new world. I am not the person today I once was, but as each day goes by, it is clear who I am becoming. My distance from all of you is more about my own personal journey and not meant to be a reflection on my love for all of you.

To those of you who took part in the effort to locate me and to those who were there when I was recovered: I want to thank you for your strength and support. In the early days of my recovery, the cards and donations gave me hope that the outside world was not such a terrible place. The money helped me believe my daughters and I would be able to survive and I would have a way at least for the time being to get by. We had left the backyard with nothing (if you don't include the hermit crabs). Each and every letter was a testament that is was okay to be free.

To El Dorado County officials: I want to thank you for your continued support and your willingness to understand the complexity of our situation and treat it with such care. To Trish Kelliher, who had the foresight to connect with the National Center for Missing and Exploited Children (NCMEC) who then were able to connect us to Transitioning Families. Those simple calls provided me a soft place to land and get my bearings. The community I landed in was full of supportive, loving people who provided the anonymity I needed. Not one person I encountered felt the need to expose our whereabouts. Even when federal cars clogged the driveways making us hard not to notice. All the officials in the know from the local sheriff's department to the FBI practiced discretion and helped keep us safe.

I want to thank Vern Pierson and staff. Throughout this journey, Vern Pierson and his staff supported me and kept me informed of the criminal proceedings with the Garridos. Vern was always willing to work closely with the mental health team supporting my family. His willingness to keep in contact with me and my team allowed me to feel important and a part of something which had very much affected my life.

Team Jaycee grew as time went on. I want to thank each and every one of you that became part of the team. To all the therapists: thanks for making therapy something we all look forward to. Each of you has brought so much insight into our lives. To Rebecca and Jane, you have taught me friendships are more than just about agreeing; people can disagree and still like each other. You both have taught me how to stand up for myself and be a strong mother to my children.

To Nancy Seltzer: I will keep this short and sweet. Your advice and support is invaluable, but it is our friendship that I value the most. I would have been lost without your guidance in dealing with the headless, nameless media. Your strength is inspirational, and I look forward to all we can accomplish with the J A Y C Foundation and, yes, I'm learning to roar a little louder.

There are so many of you who sacrificed yourself and your families to the healing of my own family. I saw the commitment it took and although none of you asked for anything, I want to thank you for your love and support. You opened your houses and hearts to me, teaching me to do the same. You all know who you are, but in case you have forgotten, thank you for Chuck E. Cheese's, the horseback riding, the Target shopping spree, fostering our beloved animals, the medical care, taking us to the snow, helping us grow as a family, but most of all helping us sometimes laugh and sometimes cry as we all figured out how to do this.

To the children of my new extended family: thanks for teaching my kids to play ball, introducing them to new music, embracing uniqueness, thanks for supporting my kids as they acclimated to this new world. And, Yes to one of you, I will work on getting you Dwight Howard's autograph! Thanks for sharing your parents with us and letting us see that being part of a family means reaching out and helping others.

And last but certainly not least, to Dr. Rebecca Bailey: You have become my mentor, my coach, and my confidante. You never treated me as a victim but instead embraced me as a friend. Together we have shared hard times and joyful times, and you have taught me to find the humor in both cases. I have found we share the same philosophy, which is, it is better to laugh and cry than to just cry. Our work together has brought insight into myself and with your help, I am growing into the adult I've always wanted to become. The words "thank you" do not begin to convey how much you mean to me. Your continued support and mentoring will always be a source of comfort and strength for me in the years to come.